THE TEZKEREH AL VAKIAT PRIVATE MEMOIRS OF THE MOGHUL EMPEROR HUMAYUN

THE TEZKEREH AL VAKIAT PRIVATE MEMOIRS OF THE MOGHUL EMPEROR HUMAYUN

JAWHAR

Published by

FacsiMile Publisher
12 Pragati Market
Ashok Vihar, Ph-2
Delhi - 110052, India
Phone: 011-47034999
Email: www.facsimilepublishers.com
info@facsimilepublishers.com

Distribution Network
gyanbooks.com
India, USA, Canada, UK, Australia

ISBN: 978-93-3348-089-5 (PB)
First Published, 1832

2nd Impression 2026

Printed at: Gyan Press, Delhi.

THE TEZKEREH AL VAKIAT PRIVATE MEMOIRS OF THE MOGHUL EMPEROR HUMAYUN
Author: JAWHAR

THE

TEZKEREH AL VAKIAT,

OR

PRIVATE MEMOIRS

OF THE

MOGHUL EMPEROR HUMAYUN,

WRITTEN IN THE PERSIAN LANGUAGE BY

JOUHER,

A CONFIDENTIAL DOMESTIC OF HIS MAJESTY;

TRANSLATED BY

MAJOR CHARLES STEWART,

OF THE HONOURABLE EAST INDIA COMPANY'S SERVICE,

M. R. A. S. &c. &c.

LONDON:

PRINTED FOR THE ORIENTAL TRANSLATION FUND

OF GREAT BRITAIN AND IRELAND.

SOLD BY

JOHN MURRAY, ALBEMARLE-STREET; AND PARBURY, ALLEN, AND CO. LEADENHALL-STREET.

M.DCCC.XXXII.

TO

THE RIGHT HONOURABLE

THE

EARL OF MUNSTER,

VISCOUNT FITZ-CLARENCE, BARON TEWKESBURY,

&c. &c. &c.

My Lord,

I have the honour to dedicate to your Lordship the Memoirs of Humāyūn, Emperor of Hindūstan; the vicissitudes of whose reign bear a great resemblance to those of our Royal Stuart family, and of the late Bourbon dynasty.

It affords me great pleasure to have an opportunity of dedicating these pages to a Personage who, from his own knowledge of the Oriental tongues, can duly appreciate the difficulties of clothing in European language the ideas and idioms of the natives of Persia and Hindūstān.

That you may long continue to support that praise-worthy Institution, of which you are the Founder, is the sincere wish of,

Your Lordship's

Most obedient, very humble Servant,

CHARLES STEWART.

Royal Crescent, Bath,
March 1*st*. 1832.

PREFACE.

During the period I was engaged in translating the Memoirs of the Emperor Timūr, I received, from my friend Major William Yule, a Persian manuscript, containing Private Memoirs of the Emperor Humāyūn, son of the celebrated Baber, and father of the no less famous Akber, sixth in descent from Timūr, and cotemporary with our King Henry VIII. with a recommendation that I should translate it. In compliance with my friend's recommendation, and at the request of the Oriental Translation Committee, I have undertaken the task.

As the Author of this Work was not a learned person, it has no claims to erudition; I have therefore not thought it requisite to give any part of the original text; and although, in conformity to the practice of the times, he has ornamented his book with various quotations from the *Korān*, with many passages from Persian poets, and historical anecdotes, I have not taken the trouble of following him in these his prolix digressions.

This book being written with the greatest sincerity and naïveté, sometimes to the disparagement of his hero, I have no doubt of its authenticity. The manuscript was purchased at Lucknow, the capital of Oude, and is, I believe, the only copy *now* in England: it is a large octavo volume, written in the common hand, and is about a century old.

The Anglo-orthography of this work is nearly the same as that of the Memoirs of Timūr, viz. a free use of the Persian letters; and the short e, representing the vowel *zubber* of that language.

I take this opportunity of declaring that I have scarcely ever met with an idea in any European poet, or a passage in any historian, that I have not found a parallel to it in Oriental writers. I must also request the readers who are inclined to criticise the style of this work, or my other Translations, that they will previously compare them with English books of the *same period*, not with those of the present day.

CHARLES STEWART.

P. S. I beg leave to add, that the book mentioned in my Preface to the Memoirs of Timūr should have been *Ajaib al Mukdūr*, "Wonders of Destiny," instead of *Ajaib al Mukhlūkāt*.

INTRODUCTION.

Humāyūn, Emperor of Hindūstān, was the son of Baber, son of Omer Shykh, son of Abū Saied, son of Muhammed Myrzā, son of Myran Hussyn, son of Timūr.

His descendants, or successors, were the Emperors Akber, Jehangyr, Shāh Jehān, Aalumgyr-Aurungzyb, Behadur Shāh, Ferrukhsyr, Muhammed, Ahmed, Aalumgyr II. Shāh Aalum, Akber II.

Humāyūn was born at Kabul (A. H. 913, A. D. 1508), being the same year in which his father had taken the title of Padshāh, the second brother was named Kamrān, the third Hindal, the fourth Askery: they all bore the title of Myrzā (Prince) *following* their names, and will make a conspicuous figure in this history.*

When Baber invaded Hindūstān (A. H. 932, A. D. 1525), he gave the command of the right wing of his army to Humāyūn, and he was the first general that engaged the Afghans. After the battle of Paniput he was sent on to secure the city of Agra, and the treasures of Sultān Ibrahīm; he also commanded the army sent against the combined forces of the chiefs possessing the country on the eastward of the Ganges: in all of which measures he succeeded, and was rewarded by his father with a present of one crore and seventy laks of dāms,† and a palace at Agra with all its contents. He afterwards took the city of Joanpūr, and then joined the imperial army previous

* As all Muhammedan names have meanings, I will explain that, Humāyūn signifies *Auspicious*, Kamrān *Successful*, Hindal *Indian*, Askery *Born in Camp:* he was probably illegitimate, as his birth is not mentioned in the portion we have of Baber's Memoirs.

† Forty of which make a rupee.

to the bloody battle fought with the Hindū Princes near Biana, in which he highly distinguished himself.

It has been deemed requisite to state these circumstances, because the Memoirs do not commence till his mounting the throne; and he has been accused of want of energy as a monarch; nay, it has been even said, that if he had been a worse man, he would have been a greater king. See Memoirs of the Emperor Baber, by William Erskine, Esq. London, 1826, and Dow's History of Hindūstān.

As the Author has seldom inserted any dates, I have been under the necessity of supplying them from other sources.

P. S. Although the dynasty of Timūr are in India called Moghuls, the family do not acknowledge themselves to be so; they are properly *Jagtay Tūrks*, of a very superior clan to the Moghuls or Tartars; but in order to discriminate them from the Turks of Constantinople, the former title has been continued to them both in this work and in the Memoirs of Timūr.

It is necessary also to observe here that the Tukhti Soleymān mentioned in the XIVth Chapter is *not* the Persepolis of the Greeks: I have not been able to discover the European name of it.

MEMOIRS OF HUMĀYŪN.

PREFACE.

In the Name of the Most Merciful God,

Glory be to God, the Lord of all Worlds, Praise and benedictions be also on his Prophet, and on all his descendants and companions;—

The dedication of this illustrious volume, is in the name of the Emperor, the Asylum of the world, the Just monarch, the Redresser of grievances, the Supporter of Church and State, Defender of the faith, Muhammed Humāyūn, the victorious Prince; may God illuminate his resting place, and perpetuate his kingdom;—

(Here follow some Persian verses, which are omitted in the translation.)

Thus saith the humble servant of the Court, the Asylum of mankind, Jouher, having had the good fortune, while still a youth, to be admitted into the service of his Majesty Humāyūn, and having continued in it till his death, I was at all times, and in all situations, in constant attendance on the royal person; it therefore occurred to me as desirable that I should write a narrative of all the events to which I had been an eye witness, that it may remain as a record of the past interesting occurrences; I have endeavoured to explain them to the best of my humble ability, although in a style very inferior to the dignity of the subject. I commenced this work in the year 995 (A.D. 1587), and have named it the Tezkereh al Vakiāt, *Relation of Occurrences.**

* Although the Author does not here mention the situation he held, he afterwards explains that he was the Aftabchy or *Ewer bearer,* an office formerly well known in all the courts of Europe, and still to be found in the establishment of our King's household.

It is not my intention however to narrate *all* the occurrences which have taken place during the late reign, but shall confine myself to those operations in which his Majesty was personally concerned; I shall therefore commence this work with Humāyūn's ascending the throne, and shall nearly conclude with his return from Persia and his regaining the sovereignty; I shall further explain with what fortitude and perseverance the late Emperor encountered so many hardships and difficulties, and through the favour of Almighty God, thereby recovered his dominions, in the hope that this book may hand down the name of the Author to posterity, and inform mankind of these extraordinary events.

MEMOIRS OF HUMĀYŪN.

CHAPTER I.

Of the death of the Emperor Zehyr-ad-dyn Muhammed Baber, (whose soul dwelleth in Paradise) and the mounting the throne by his son Nesyr-ad-dyn Muhammed Humāyūn.* A. H. 937.—A. D. 1530.

(Here some verses from the Korān are introduced.)

The first events that occurred, after his Majesty's succession to the throne, were the rebellions of Byn and Bayezid, Afghāns, and of Mahmūd Lody, in the eastern provinces of the empire; in consequence of which his Majesty led his army (from Callinger) towards Joanpūr, and, having encamped on the banks of the river Goompty, fought and defeated the rebels with great slaughter, A. H. 938. After this victory his Majesty proceeded against the strong fortress of Chunar, which was commanded by Jelal Khān, the son of the celebrated Shyr Khān, who after a siege of four months made his submission, and peace was concluded on the condition of a party of Afghāns commanded by Abdal Rashid, second son of Shyr, joining the King's army, which in consequence marched to Agra, the capital of the Moghuls. *(See History of Bengal, page* 138.)

* Zehyr-ad-dyn and Nesyr-ad-dyn are synonimous, signifying the Support of Religion: every Mussulmān may take the surname of Muhammed.

CHAPTER II.

Account of his Majesty's expedition to Gujerāt, and the conquest of that province. A. H. 940.—A. D. 1533.

When the royal army approached the fortress of Chētūr on its way to Gujerāt, a letter was received from Sultān Behāder of Gujerāt representing that he had laid siege to Chētūr, and hoped very shortly to subdue the *Infidels* and exalt the fame of the *Mussulmān* faith, and therefore hoped his Majesty would not interfere.

The King, from his attachment to the true faith and his heroical spirit, complied with the request; and having halted his troops waited till the fort was taken, after which Sultān Behāder having returned to his own dominions, his Majesty then continued his march till he reached the village of Mury, a dependency of the district of Burhānpūr.

Here he was opposed by the army of Sultān Behāder; on which his Majesty consulted with his chiefs how he should fight the enemy; each of the generals gave his opinion according to the best of his ability; at length the King issued orders that his troops should surround the army of the Sultān, and cut off all their supplies; in consequence of this determination several of the Moghul chieftains were detached, and ordered to act as *Cossacs*, by preventing any grain or other provisions from entering the enemy's camp: this mode of warfare continued for nearly three months, when provisions became so scarce that the enemy were obliged to live on horseflesh, and suffered great distress; during this time skirmishes took place daily between the advanced parties.

One night a dreadful noise and tumult was heard in the enemy's camp; soon after which Ala Kūly, the chief engineer, came to his Majesty's tent door, and when questioned respecting the cause of the uproar, represented that, he supposed the enemy were retreating, and that Rūmy Khān, the commandant of their artillery, had burst his two large guns, called Lyly and Mujenūn; during this conversation a person arrived from the enemy's camp, and informed his Majesty that Sultān Behāder with his army had taken flight, on which his Majesty returned thanks to the Almighty. The King then mounted his horse and pursued the Sultān, but on his way was joined by Rūmy Khān, who, having deserted from the enemy, came and offered his services.

Intelligence having been brought that Sultān Behāder had taken refuge in the fortress of Mundū, in the province of Malwa, the victorious army proceeded towards that place, and laid siege to the fort; after some time the Sultān again made his escape, and shut himself up in the strong fortress of Chunpanyr. In the mean time the royal army having taken possession of Mundū found much plunder and treasure; but his Majesty not paying any attention to such trifles eagerly pursued the Sultān, and having arrived at Chunpanyr, the capital of Gujerāt, laid siege to it.* After the siege had been carried on for a considerable time, a person waited on his Majesty, and in private informed him, that he could lead the troops across the summit of a mountain to a place which completely commanded the fortress: the King placing confidence in this representation, selected a small body of brave men, and accompanied by two drummers and a trumpeter secretly left the camp, and, having by a difficult pathway ascended the mountain, got into the fort. He then ordered the drummers to beat and the trumpeter to sound, on which the different chiefs made a simultaneous attack on all the bastions, and, the enemy finding themselves thus beset, called out for quarter; in the mean time some of the garrison made their escape, and Sultān Behāder fled to Cambay: thus his Majesty got possession of this celebrated city with all its stores, but could not discover the treasure and jewels.

After a few days one of the Sultān's principal officers, named Aalum Khān, came to pay his respects to his Majesty; on which occasion several of the counsellors advised his being seized and put to the torture, in order to make him discover where the treasures were concealed; but the King replied, "as this personage has come to me of his own accord, it would be ungenerous to make use of force: if an object can be attained by gentleness, why have recourse to harsh measures? Do ye give orders that a banquet may be prepared, and ply him well with wine, and then put the question, where the treasures may be found."

(Here follow several Arabic and Persian verses.)

* See Dow's History of Hindūstān, vol. ii. page 144, and also Edinburgh Gazetteer.

In compliance with the King's commands a banquet was prepared; and when Aalum Khān was intoxicated they asked him respecting the treasures. Aalum Khān being highly gratified by the reception he had met with, said, that if his Majesty wished for the Sultān's wealth, he had only to order the water to be drawn off the large bath, over which they were then seated. This being reported to the King, he ordered them to collect a number of buckets and other vessels, and to empty the bath: while the people were thus employed, Aalum Khān told them that there was a more expeditious mode of doing it: he then directed them to dig under the Bath, where they discovered a drain and a plug-hole, which being opened allowed the water quickly to run off; they then found a great quantity of treasure, which was immediately divided among the army, by filling the shield of each person with materials in proportion to his rank: they afterwards discovered a well filled with gold and silver that had been melted (into ingots), which was preserved untouched by the army.

After this the King appointed Terdy Beg to the command of Chunpanyr, and prepared to set out for Cambay in pursuit of Sultān Behāder.

But the counsellors cunningly represented to his Majesty, that as he had through the grace of God obtained the objects for which he had commenced this war, viz. by defeating and expelling Sultān Behāder, and obtaining immense wealth, it would now be advisable to advance one or two years pay to the army, to keep the remaining treasure in deposit for future emergencies, and then appoint Sultān Behāder his deputy to rule the province of Gujerāt;* that such a liberal action would redound much to his fame, and would afford him leisure to look after his other dominions; more especially his presence being now required at Agra (the capital), from whence unfavourable rumours had reached them respecting the rebellion of Muhammed Zemān Sultān and some other chiefs. His Majesty was much displeased with this advice, and said, "After having subdued this valuable province by the power of my sword, shall I give it up for nothing? No; I will keep it, and add it to the kingdom of Dehly."

When the counsellors found that the King was displeased, and would not

* The most western province of British India.

listen to their advice, they instigated the Prince Askery* to march off with his division of the army, and to give out that he was going to seize upon the province of Dehly: this measure was carried into effect. About the same time the Prince Yadgār Nassir went privately to the governor of Chunpanyr, and told him that he had been sent by the King to take command of the fortress, and also possession of the treasures; but Terdy Beg refused to comply, and sent off an express to his Majesty on the subject, and to request his further orders, which were immediately sent, viz. to keep possession of the place and treasure. But when the King found that the princes and chiefs were thus confederating against him, and that his force was much reduced by the various detachments that had been sent to different places, he ordered the latter to be recalled, and proceeded towards Ahmedabad.† On the route, having received information of various insurrections, he resolved to march to his capital, where he arrived in health and safety. Sultān Behāder, finding that his Majesty had marched towards Agra, entered into a treaty with the Europeans (Portuguese) of Surat, and having through their assistance raised a force of 6000 Abyssinians or Negroes returned to Ahmedabad.

I must now revert to the insurrection which took place during his Majesty's expedition to Gujerāt. During the period that the King was employed in subduing the province of Gujerāt, Muhammed Zemān Sultān, (a descendant of Timūr,‡ and favourite of the late Emperor) taking advantage of his Majesty's absence, gained possession of the countries situated on the north-east side of the Ganges, and fixed his own residence at Belgram, but despatched his son Aleg Myrza, with a considerable force to seize on the provinces of Joanpūr, Kurra and Manikpūr. As soon as this intelligence reached the Prince Hindal, the King's youngest brother and representative at Agra, he collected an army and marched to Canouge; in consequence of this event Sultān Muhammed recalled his divisions and encamped with all his force on the northern bank of the Ganges to oppose the royal troops: in this situation the contending armies remained for some time. At length the emissaries of Hindal discovered a ford about ten miles above Canouge, the Prince imme-

* He was a natural brother of the King's, and is frequently mentioned in Baber's Memoirs.

† Now the capital of Gujerāt, taken by the English A. D. 1780.

‡ He was a son of the celebrated Sultān Hussyn of Herat. See Catalogue of Tippoo's Library.

diately took advantage of this circumstance, and having ordered that his camp should remain standing, marched quietly in the night, and without being perceived by the rebels crossed the river with all his troops.

As soon as the day broke the two armies drew up in order of battle; but just as the engagement was about to commence a very violent storm from the north-west arose, and raised such a dust that the sky was obscured, and blew with so much force in the faces of the rebels that they could not distinguish friend from foe; in consequence of which they took to flight, and proceeded towards Joanpūr. The Prince Hindal having thus gained possession of the district of Belgram followed the enemy, and again came up with them in the vicinity of Oude; but, as the force of the two armies were now nearly equal, a considerable time was lost in skirmishing, and endeavouring to gain the advantage of each other. At length Muhammed Sultān, having received information that the King was returned in health and safety to his capital, was afraid to contend any longer, and fled with all his family towards Couch Behar, which adjoins the territory of Bengal. The Prince Hindal then proceeded to Joanpūr, and took possession of that district.

CHAPTER III.

The arrival of the King at Agra—Return of the Prince Hindal to Court—Intelligence arrives of the rebellion of Shyr Shāh in Behar—The King marches to Chunar and takes that fortress. A. H. 944.—A. D. 1537.

Some time after his Majesty had arrived in safety at his palace of Agra, the Prince Hindal and his officers returned from their expedition, and had the honour of paying their respects at the foot of the throne: they were all distinguished by honorary dresses; a sumptuous banquet was given them, and the marriage ceremony of the Prince Hindal was celebrated with great rejoicings: the Prince Askery also, in reward for his good conduct, had the district of Sumbul conferred on him, with orders to drive from thence all the partisans of the rebels. At this time his Majesty was informed that Shyr Khān, the Afghān, had taken possession of the district of Jarkund in

Behar, and by artifice had seized the strong fortress of Rhotas;* that he was then besieging Gour, the capital of Bengal, and it was expected he would very shortly take that city.

On hearing this intelligence his Majesty was much incensed, and said, "The insolence of these Afghāns exceeds all bounds; let us go and take Chunar from them." He then consulted Rūmy Khān, the engineer, (who had deserted from Sultān Behāder) what was his opinion as to the practicability of taking that fortress. Rūmy Khān replied, "If it pleased God we shall take it by force."

In short the army marched from Agra and arrived within ten miles of Chunar on the day of *Sheb berat* of A. H. 945, A. D. 1538. The engineer then deliberated how he should gain information respecting the strength and defences of the fortress, and against which of the bastions he should make his attack, or where he should run his mines; in order to effect this measure he adopted the following cruel expedient. He had a faithful Negro slave called Kelāfāt, whom he flogged in such a manner that the stripes were conspicuous on his back and limbs; he then commanded the slave to go to the Afghāns, and say that he was the servant of Rūmy Khān; but that his master having unjustly flogged him he had deserted, and had come to offer his services to them; that if he succeeded to get into the fort by these means he should minutely examine it, and then return to him, when he should be well rewarded.

Kelāfāt strictly complied with the orders he had received, went to the Afghāns, was admitted into the fort, where his wounds were dressed and cured; he then informed them that he was well skilled in engineering; that if they would employ him, he would point out to them where they should mount their guns more effectually to annoy the enemy, and would indicate to them where the fortifications required strengthening, in order to prevent Rūmy Khān from making any impression on them.

The scheme succeeded, and the deserter was allowed to examine every part of the fort.† A few nights after this having made his escape, he came

* See History of Bengal, page 139.

† In the year 1763 the English attempted to take Chunar by storm, but were repulsed: it afterwards capitulated. See Edinburgh Gazetteer.

and reported all the circumstances to his master; advised him to attack the bastion on the river side, to run a sap on the land side, and to surround the place in such a manner as to cut off all communication with the country.

In consequence of this useful information Rūmy Khān brought his great guns to bear on the bastion near the river, and appointed different batteries round the fort to various officers.

During this period Muhammed Sultān, and the other rebel chiefs formerly mentioned, came and asked forgiveness for their transgression, which his Majesty was graciously pleased to grant, and gave them suitable commands in the army.

Rūmy Khān finding that his guns did not make a proper impression on the fort, requested permission to erect a wooden battery on the river: he was ordered to take any measures he thought best to effect the end. He therefore procured three large boats, on which he formed a battery, and built up a high tower which commanded the walls of the fort. After some months, when every thing was prepared, the floating battery was impelled during the night across the river, and anchored close to the fort. A general attack was then commenced; but the besieged so well defended themselves, that the floating battery was injured, and seven hundred of the King's troops were killed, while but little impression was made on the fortress.

On the following morning the artificers were employed to repair the floating battery; but the besieged finding that his Majesty was determined on taking the place, and that they had no prospect of being relieved, agreed to surrender on condition of their lives being spared.

After the fort had, in consequence of the capitulation, been taken possession of, Rūmy Khān selected from the prisoners *three hundred* artillerymen, and cruelly ordered their hands to be cut off: his Majesty was very angry on this occasion, and said that, as the garrison had asked for quarter, it was base and improper to maim them in this manner.

As soon as this important fortress was in his Majesty's possession he gave orders for a grand banquet to be prepared, and great rejoicings to be made; he conferred a number of promotions on the officers, and bestowed honorary dresses on all the chiefs.

The King asked Rūmy Khān what he thought the best mode of securing the fort, and to whom he should entrust it; the engineer replied that no person should be allowed to approach near it, and that he did not think there was an officer in the army worthy to command it, unless it was Beg Myrek: in consequence of this advice, his Majesty appointed that officer to the command of the fortress; but the other chiefs were so much incensed at Rūmy Khān for his candid advice that they confederated together, and in a few days had a poisoned cup presented to him, which caused his death.

CHAPTER IV.

The King proceeds to Bengal, and subdues that province. A. H. 945—A. D. 1538-9.

His Majesty having taken possession of the strong fortress of Chunar, marched towards Bengal; when encamped near Benares, he made particular inquiries respecting Shyr Khān; in answer to which the Raja Buja of Benares informed him that Shyr was then besieging Gour, the capital of Bengal, and expected every day to take it, and probably was ere this time in possession of the whole province. His Majesty replied, that in order to prevent the Afghāns uniting, he would go and take the fortress of Rhotas* from them. In short the royal army marched towards the district of *Bherkund* (Jarkund), but when they had reached the river Soane, intelligence was brought that Shyr Khān had taken the city of Gour, and intended to remove all the treasures to the fort of Rhotas.

His Majesty now determined to detach the Prince Hindal and Yadgār Myrza to secure Dehly and Agra, while he himself proceeded towards Bengal. In consequence of this resolution, these two princes were detached with their respective forces to assume the command of the above mentioned provinces, and his Majesty continued his route towards *Bherkund,* but at the same time sent forward Hussyn, the Tūrkumān, as his ambassador to Shyr Khān, with the following message, viz. "that he should immediately send to his Majesty the *umbrella, the throne*, and the treasure of Bengal, and that he should evacuate the fort of Rhotas, and give up possession of the

* See Edinburgh Gazetteer, or History of Bengal.

territory he had taken; in exchange for which he might have the fort of Chunar, the city of Joanpūr, and any other place he chose."

Shyr Khān received the ambassador graciously; but replied, "that, it having cost him five or six years toil to subdue Bengal, with the loss of a great number of his soldiers, it was impossible he could resign that conquest." When the ambassador returned with this message, he further explained to his Majesty that Shyr Khān, attended by a large force, was proceeding by the hill road with all the treasures towards Rhotas.

When the royal army arrived at Mūneah (situated at the junction of the Soane with the Ganges), Syed Mahmūd, the expelled king of Bengal, joined the camp,* having been severely wounded while making his escape. He represented to his Majesty that he had yet several granaries and stores in Bengal sufficient for many armies, and urged his Majesty to proceed thither.

Humāyūn received the unfortunate monarch with great courtesy; encouraged him to keep up his spirits, and assured him he would reinstate him in his kingdom of Bengal.

From Mūneah the King detached Jehangyr Kūly with a large force to precede the army, and to gain possession of the strong passes of Terryagurhy and Sikryagurhy.

In compliance with these orders Jehangyr Kūly made several forced marches; but, on his arrival in the vicinity of the passes, found that Jelal Khān, son of Shyr Khān, had strongly fortified them, and was encamped there with a large force.

The royal army was therefore obliged to halt; and while they were endeavouring to explore a road through the hills, Jelal Khān made a sally; surprised the camp, and killed a number of brave officers and men. On this event the advanced party retreated, and joined the main body at Colgong: while at this place a very heavy rain fell for several days, which compelled the King to halt, during which time Hajy Muhammed Beg was sent forward to explore the passes and procure further intelligence.

When the Hajy reached the pass he obtained information that Shyr Khān had written to his son Jelal, that all the treasures of Bengal being

* See History of Bengal, page 121.

now secured, he might evacuate the passes, and permit the Moghuls to enter that province, whilst some means might be devised to surround and entrap them. In obedience to this order Jelal immediately commenced his retreat.

On receiving this unexpected intelligence the Hajy sent back two of his officers to congratulate his Majesty on the success of his arms, and on his being master of the passes. On obtaining this information the King moved forward with the whole army, and in four days with little difficulty took possession of Gour, the capital of Bengal, and drove away all the Afghāns.*

After cleansing and repairing the city, the first act of his Majesty was to divide the province into Jagyrs among his officers; after which he very unaccountably shut himself up for a considerable time in his *Haram*, and abandoned himself to every kind of indulgence and luxury.

While the King had thus for several months given himself up to pleasure and indolence, information was at length conveyed to him that Shyr Khān had killed seven hundred Moghuls, had laid siege to the fortress of Chunar, and taken the city of Benares; and had also sent forward an army along the banks of the Ganges to take Canouge; that he had, further, seized the families of several of the officers, and sent them prisoners to Rhotas.

When his Majesty was informed of these inauspicious events, he affected not to believe them, and said, "it was impossible that Shyr Khān should have dared to do so." At length, his Majesty, being convinced of the truth of the intelligence, called a general assembly of his officers, and consulted with them what was advisable to be done, and whom he should leave in charge of Bengal: the officers replied, "that he might promote and appoint to that honour whomsoever he thought best fitted for it." The King then said, "Zahid Beg has often urged me to promote him: I will now appoint him governor of Bengal, and leave with him several other officers with their quotas of troops."

Zahid Beg, being present, and not liking Bengal, said, "What! could you find no other place to kill me in than Bengal?" On hearing this speech, the King was very angry, and said, "I must put this scoundrel to death." Zahid Beg immediately rose and left the assembly.

It is requisite to observe that the cause of this officer's presumption was

* See History of Bengal, page 123.

his being married to a sister of *Bykē Begum*, one of the King's concubines. He therefore immediately went to claim the protection of the Begum, who strongly interceded for his pardon; begged the King to forgive him, and leave him in charge of Bengal: but his Majesty positively refused, and said, "he would put him to death." On this the Begum sent a message to Zahid Beg, informing him that she had in vain tried to obtain his pardon; he had better therefore look to himself. On this hint the culprit resolved to make his escape; and having prevailed on two other officers to join him, fled towards Agra, where having arrived in safety, they took refuge with the Prince Hindal.

When the assembly broke up, his Majesty ordered Khān Khānān Ludy to take the command of the advanced guard and proceed to Mongier, there to wait the arrival of the main body: these orders were duly complied with, and Khān Khānān having reached Mongier, halted there.

In the mean time, the King having settled all the affairs of Bengal, appointed Jehangyr Kūly to be governor, and marched towards Mongier; but previous to his arrival there, he received intelligence that the rebel, Shyr Khān, had sent a detachment which had come unexpectedly on Mongier, had burnt the gates of the town, and had taken Khān Khānān prisoner,* and sent him off to Shyr Khān.

This event gave the King great uneasiness; he therefore sent for the Prince Askery, his best general, and offered him any thing he chose to ask, provided he could deliver him from the present calamity: the Prince replied that he would consult with his officers, and then inform his Majesty. Having assembled his officers, the Prince communicated to them the King's offer. After some delay they said, "what are the wishes of your Highness?" he replied, "I should wish for money; for some of the valuable manufactures of Bengal; for some young elephants, and a few *eunuchs*."† The officers were quite astonished at this answer; and the Prince seeing that they were dissatisfied, insisted upon their giving their sentiments frankly: they at

* As this personage was an Afghān nobleman, it is more probable that he carried on a treasonable correspondence with Shyr Khān.

† In the Ayeen Akberry we find that Bengal, especially the district of Silhet, supplied the market with eunuchs. See vol. i. page 10.

length said, "the fact is, the King is now in hostility with Shyr Khān, and placed in a very perilous situation, from whence nothing but our bravery and devotion can extricate him, let us, therefore, demand from him something of importance. In the first place, an augmentation of each of our corps, and an increase of allowance; secondly, a large sum in ready money: if he shall comply with these terms, we will be answerable that Shyr Khān shall not injure him." Askery approved of this counsel, and represented it to his Majesty, who immediately agreed to the terms; gave them a sum of money, and various presents; he also sent to them a reinforcement of brave men and distinguished officers. He then ordered the Prince to proceed towards the enemy, to force his way through the passes, and wait for the coming up of the main body at Colgong; but in the mean time to send all the information he could obtain respecting the movements of Shyr Khān, who had now taken the title of *Shāh* (King). Askery complied with these orders, and sent intelligence from Colgong that Shyr Shāh was at the same time besieging Chunar and Joanpūr, and had actually taken possession of all the country as far as Canouge; further, that he was collecting a large army in the vicinity of Rhotas, and had completely blocked up the road to the western provinces.

On receipt of this bad news the King advanced rapidly to the vicinity of Mongier, on the northern side of the river; and while encamped there was waited on by the Prince Askery, and the officers of the advance guard.

The King then summoned a general council of all the Chiefs, and demanded their opinion whether he should cross the Ganges, or continue his route on the northern bank of the river; many of the chiefs advised that the army should continue on the northern bank, and proceed direct to Joanpūr, where, being refreshed and recruited, they might then proceed towards any object that might appear advisable.

Muvyd Beg, in whom his Majesty unfortunately placed too much confidence, was of a different opinion, and represented that if the army did not pass the river and proceed by the high road, Shyr Khān would suppose the King was afraid of him, according to the proverb, "when fate descends the eyes of prudence become blind;" and the advice of Muvyd Beg was adopted.*

* It appears extraordinary why the high road between Benares and Gour should have been

In short, the army crossed the river and marched on till it reached Mūneah, at the mouth of the Soane, where is situated the tomb of the celebrated Sūfy Saint Yehy. Here a crier was sent round the camp to proclaim that the soldiers should put on their armour, and be on their guard, as the enemy might be hourly expected; in fact on the next day some of them appeared, and a skirmish took place between the advanced parties.

The day following, while we were preparing to march, news was brought that the enemy had seized the boats, which were laden with all the great guns that had been used at the siege of Chunar. This intelligence much vexed his Majesty; but he gave orders to proceed in battle array.

On the fourth day, while we were encamped near the village of Chowsar,* the army of Shyr Shāh, having made a forced march, came in sight. His Majesty then consulted with the Chiefs what was proper to be done. Kasim Hussyn said, " that, as the enemy had come thirty-six miles that day, and their horses were much tired, while ours were quite fresh, it was advisable to attack them immediately, and let us see to whom God would give the victory."

The King approved this measure; but Muvyd Beg was again of a contrary opinion to the other officers, and said, " there was no necessity for hurry or perturbation;" to which his Majesty having at length agreed, the army encamped; but the troops were disheartened.

Shyr Khān also encamped, but threw up an entrenchment around his camp. In this situation the armies remained for nearly two months; but skirmishing took place daily between the pickets, and a number of brave men were killed on both sides.

At this juncture the rains set in with great violence, and the camp of Shyr Khān was under water; in consequence of which he changed his ground, and encamped on the skirts of a hill five or six miles to the westward; but the skirmishing still continued, till at length it was thought advisable to enter into a treaty with the enemy and make peace.

conducted on the south side of the Ganges. The King certainly owed his misfortune to having made use of it, instead of passing by Hajypūr.

* A battle was fought here in 1764 between the British and the army of Shujā ad Dowlā. It is generally called the battle of Buxar.

In consequence of this determination, the very respectable and reverend Shykh Khelyl, who was descended from the celebrated saint, Feryd *Sheker-gunjy*, was sent to Shyr Khān for the purpose of settling the treaty. Shyr Khān agreed to make peace on condition of Chunar with its district being given up to him.

At first the King would not consent to this measure, but at length was obliged to comply with his insolent demands, and peace was accordingly concluded.

CHAPTER V.

Of the night attack made by Shyr Khān, and its consequences. A. H. 946—A. D. 1539.

As soon as the peace was concluded, the treacherous Shyr Khān summoned his principal officers, and said to them, "is there any of you brave enough to go and storm the Moghul camp?" At first not one of the Afghān officers would undertake the task. At length a person called Khuās Khān said, "if he would give him a detachment of good soldiers and a a number of war elephants, he would attempt it, and exert himself to the utmost;" adding, "this is a business of chance; but let us see to whom 'God will give the victory.'"

Shyr Khān was much pleased with Khuās Khān's proposal, and gave him his choice of all the troops and several war elephants; but although the detachment marched from the camp at ten o'clock of the morning, the artful general loitered about till night. In the mean time, Shykh Khelyl sent off a messenger to his Majesty, cautioning him to be on his guard; but "when fate descends, caution is in vain."

(Here follows a long story taken from the history of Muhammed on the fatal effects of presumption.)

The King would not believe the information, or that Shyr Khān would be guilty of such a breach of honour or religion, and passed the night without taking any precautions; but just as the sun rose next morning, the Afghāns entered the rear of our encampment; made a dreadful uproar, and caused the greatest confusion both among the troops and followers. His Majesty on hearing the noise ordered the kettle-drums to be beaten, and in a short time about three hundred cavalry assembled around him. In a few minutes one of the enemy's war elephants approached; on which his Majesty made a sign to Myr Bejkē, who was celebrated for his valour, and who, with his two sons, Gurk Aly and Tetta Beg, one of whom carried the King's double-barrelled gun and the other the royal spear, to attack the elephant; but as none of them had the heart to do it, his Majesty snatched the spear from the hand of Gurk Aly, spurred on his horse, and struck the elephant with such force on the forehead that he could not draw out the spear again: in the mean time an archer who was seated on the elephant discharged an arrow, which wounded the King in the arm, and the enemy began to surround him. His Majesty then called to his troops to advance and charge the enemy, but no one obeyed; and the Afghāns having succeeded in throwing every thing into confusion, one of the King's followers came up, seized his bridle, and said "there is no time to be lost; when your friends forsake you, flight is the only remedy." The King then proceeded to the bank of the river, and although followed by one of his own elephants, he urged his horse into the stream,* but in a short time the horse sunk. On seeing this event a *water carrier* who had distended his leathern bag (musek) with air, offered it to his Majesty, who by means of the bag swam the river. On reaching the northern bank he asked the man his name; he said, "Nizam:" the King replied, "I will make your name as celebrated as that of Nizam-addyn-Aulia (a famous saint), and you shall sit on my throne."

On this memorable day a great number of the royal troops were killed, and an equal number drowned in attempting to cross the Ganges;† in short his Majesty, having escaped this dreadful danger, proceeded towards Agra.

In a little time the King received intelligence that Myr Feryd Gūr was pursuing him from the eastward, and that Shāh Muhammed Afghān was encamped in his front, and determined to prevent his progress. On hearing this bad news the troops were very much discouraged, and inclined to desert their standards.

At length *Rajah Perbehān* represented, that if his Majesty would permit

* Baber tells us in his Memoirs that he swam his horse across the Ganges in several places, but it was probably in the dry season.

† In the History of Hindūstān the number is stated at 8000.

him, he would undertake with his own troops to stop Fëryd Gūr; in the mean time the King might continue his march and encounter his enemies. These measures were approved, and the army advanced; upon which the Afghāns retreated, and left the road open.

After a number of marches the royal army arrived at Calpy,* where the governor, the son of Kasim Kerāchy, had prepared a number of presents for the King, but by the shameful advice of his father, who commanded one of the divisions of the army, only offered a few trifling articles. On hearing of this circumstance his Majesty would not accept any of them but an embroidered saddle, which he said he would take for his brother Kamrān.

From Calpy the army continued its march till it reached Agra, in the vicinity of which place the Prince Kamrān was encamped in a garden called the Zer Afshān (*scattering gold*): when the Prince heard of his Majesty's approach he came out to meet him; and the King having alighted from his horse embraced him; after which they went and sat in the Prince's tent. After some time Kamrān said, " as your Majesty has now arrived in safety, and regained possession of your throne, I request you will forgive our younger brother, the Prince Hindal, his improper conduct for my sake."† The King replied, " I forgive him *at your request:* write to him that he may come to court in safety."

Soon after the King had remounted his throne, the water carrier who had enabled him to swim the Ganges paid his respects; and his Majesty remembering his royal promise, seated him for two hours upon the throne, and desired him to ask for whatever he wished.

Some days afterwards the King held a public court at the Stone Palace in the garden of the late Emperor Baber, at which were present all the Princes and Nobles.

When the assembly were seated, the King, turning to his brother Kamrān, said, " tell me honestly what was the reason of Hindal rebelling against me." Kamrān did not answer his Majesty; but addressing Hindal, asked, " how did it happen that, instead of sending assistance to his Majesty, you

* A large town situated on the south bank of the river Jumna.

† On learning Humāyūn's defeat he had seized on some of the provinces in his own name, and was then at Alūr.

deserted him in his distress?" Hindal was much ashamed; laid the blame on his evil advisers, and pleaded his own youth and inexperience; acknowledged his fault, and asked forgiveness. The King replied, "very well, as you now repent and have asked pardon, I forgive you, but it is at the request of your brother; I hope this will be a warning to you never to listen to the insidious advice of evil-minded persons; don't you recollect the story of the discord that took place among the companions of the prophet in consequence of the malicious advice of some of his slanderers." He then added, "what has passed, has passed, let us think no more of it, but let us be unanimous and devise means to repel Shyr Shāh and the Afghāns, who after concluding peace with me at Chowsar, acted treacherously, attacked me at night, and have now gained possession of all my territory as far as Canouge."

The Princes and Nobles replied, "by the grace of God, and the good fortune of your Majesty, we will henceforward evince our bravery and attachment in such a manner as completely to subdue all your enemies." Soon after this conversation the prayer for success was read, and his Majesty commanded that at the end of the month Zykād the royal tents should be pitched in the garden of Zer Afshān, as the preliminary of our marching against the enemy.

The Prince Kamrān entreated that the King would remain in his capital, and permit him to command the army, and promised that he would give a good account of the Afghāns, but the King replied, "No, Shyr Khān defeated me, and I will have my revenge of him, do you remain here;" in short it was determined that the King should lead the army in person, and the Prince continue in charge of Agra.

CHAPTER VI.

The King marches to meet the enemy and is defeated. Rebellion of the Prince Kamrān. A. H. 947. A. D. 1540.

The following day the King, attended by the whole army, left the city and encamped on the plains of Abhypūr; he then reviewed and mustered the troops, the number of which amounted to to 90,000 cavalry, but as some of them were not properly equipped his Majesty ordered them to be well supplied from the arsenal.* He also conferred honorary dresses and other marks of distinction on all the principal officers, and omitted nothing to rouse the spirits and encourage the soldiers for the ensuing campaign. After a few days march, the army reached Canouge, which is situated on the western bank of the Ganges, and here learned that Shyr Khān was encamped on the other side of the river; at this time an express arrived from *Raja Perbehān of Aroul* offering to join him with his troops, provided the King would meet him at *Pute.* His Majesty, however, would not agree to this measure, but gave orders for the army to cross the river at Canouge.

It was on the 10th day of the month Muharrem, that the army clothed in armour, with kettle drums beating and trumpets sounding, passed the Ganges, the right was commanded by the Prince Hindal, and was opposed to Jelal the son of Shyr Khān; the left was led by the Prince Askery, and was opposed by Khuās Khān, and the center under the orders of his Majesty advanced against the main body of the Afghāns, when a fierce battle ensued beyond the powers of description.

Here follow some Persian verses.

After the battle had raged for some time, information was brought to his Majesty that the Prince Hindal had discomfited the Afghāns opposed to him, but that the left under Askery was compelled to retreat; Myrza Hyder represented that in order to let the fugitives pass, it was requisite to loose the chains of the carriages which formed a barricade in front of the center, his Majesty unfortunately complied with this advice, and the chains, being unloosed, the runaways passed through the line of carriages in files.

During this time an Afghān clothed in black, advanced and struck the king's horse on the forehead with a spear, on which the animal turned round and became unmanageable.

Here follow several verses of the Korān, to prove we cannot contend with fate.

His Majesty afterwards related, that as soon as he could controul his horse he saw the Afghāns employed in plundering the carriages, and wished to have charged them, but some person caught the reins of the steed, and led

* N. B. The soldiers found their own horses and arms, but this was a gratuitous act of his Majesty.

him to the bank of the river. Here, while undetermined how to act, he saw an old elephant which had belonged to the late Emperor, he called to the driver to bring the elephant to him, who did so, he then mounted, and asked a eunuch who was in the *Howdah*, what was his name, he replied "Kafūr;" his Majesty then ordered the driver to carry him across the river, but the fellow refused, and said the elephant would be drowned, on which the eunuch whispered, that he suspected the driver wished to carry them over to the enemy, it would therefore be advisable to take off the fellow's head; the King said, "how shall we then make the elephant cross the river;" the eunuch replied, "that he understood something of driving an elephant,"* upon hearing this, his Majesty drew his sword and so wounded the driver that he fell off into the water, and the eunuch stepped down from the Howdah on the neck of the animal, and caused him to pass the river; his Majesty further related, that when he arrived near the bank, it was so steep that he could not find a place to ascend, at length some of the camp colour men, who were on the look out for him, tied their turbans together, and throwing an end of the cloth to him, he with some difficulty climbed up, they then brought him a horse on which he mounted and proceeded towards Agra, the King further added, "that the persons who commanded the colour-men were two brothers who seemed so affectionate to each other, that it aroused a sympathy in my breast, and I became very anxious for the safety of my brother Hindal and my other connections. In about an hour, the arrow of my prayer hit the butt of consent, for my dear brother came and paid his respects, on which I returned thanks to the Almighty God, by whose single command of *Be*! the whole universe was instantly produced."†

O my friends, although his Majesty was in some respects unfortunate, as who can contend against fate; still you see his prayers were accepted.

Here follows a verse of the Korān, which is followed by three anecdotes taken from the ecclesiastical (Muhammedan) history, to prove that good fortune and adversity, depend upon times and seasons.

* The Birman princes always guided their own elephants, and it appears by the Lucknow Newspapers, that the King of Oude now does it, formerly it would have been reckoned derogatory to a great man.

† The Korān states that when the Almighty created the Universe, he merely said Kūn, *Be*, and it was.

In short the King having been joined by the Princes Hindal and Askery and the Myrzās Yadgār Nasir, &c. proceeded joyfully towards Agra, when they reached the village of Bhyngāng, the peasants who were in the habit of plundering a defeated army, stopped up the road, and one of them wounded Myrzā Yadgār with an arrow, on which the Myrzā* said to the Prince Askery, "do you go on and punish these villagers, while I stop to dress my wound." The Prince was displeased at this request, and gave the Myrzā some abuse, on which the other retorted in harsher language, and the Prince struck him three times with his horsewhip, which was returned with interest on the other side.

When intelligence of this unpleasant fracas reached the King, he said, "they had better have vented their spite on the robbers than on each other, what has happened cannot be recalled, but let us hear no more of it."

In short the King reached Agra in safety, and alighted at the house of *Syed Rafia Addyn* (a religious person), who immediately brought forward bread and melons, and whatever else was ready for his Majesty's breakfast, but the King ordered the Prince Hindal and all the servants to go into the Fort and to bring out his mother and family, and their domestics, also the treasures and stores.

It now becomes requisite to mention the strange conduct of the Prince Kamrān. It has been stated that when the King marched from Agra, he left his brother in charge of the city and commander of the province; a short time after the departure of the army, the Prince was taken ill, and supposing that the climate disagreed with him, he prevailed on several of the officers of government to accompany him to Lahore, where he recommenced his insidious conduct, which shall be further explained.

After the King had refreshed himself, his host the *Syed* entered into a religious discourse with him, and said, "the affairs of this world are sometimes like a running stream, and at other times like a standing pool! it is, therefore, advisable that your Majesty should now abandon this place."

* At this period a number of the descendants of Timūr and a few of Jengyz Khān had found their way into Hindūstān and all took the title of Myrzā; but although this ought to follow the name, it is frequently not attended to, and in this work it often precedes the name, as Myrzā Yadgār, &c. this person was married to an aunt of the King's.

He then presented a handsomely caparisoned horse, and gave the King his blessing.

The King having mounted proceeded towards the town of Futtypūr Sikry, on the march he was joined by the Prince Hindal, who, after paying his respects, presented a rich dagger and inlaid sword, which he had brought from the arsenal of Agra. The first day the King halted in the garden of the late Emperor Baber, but while he was seated there an arrow came from the hill of Sikry, two of the attendants were immediately sent up the hill to discover who was the perpretator of this act, but they both soon returned severely wounded without seeing any body.

His Majesty, suspecting some treachery might be intended, again mounted his horse and proceeded towards the village of Chuneh; at this time, besides the domestics, there were but a few officers in attendance, one of these however, named Fakher Aly, had the insolence to precede the King, on which his Majesty became very angry, and said to him, " it was by *your* advice that I crossed the Ganges (previous to the late battle) I wish you had been killed there, how dare you presume to go before me;" in consequence Fakher Aly turned round his horse, made his obeisance, and fell into the rear of the troop.

When the King had safely arrived at Chuneh, and was halted on the bank of the Kenbyr river, the Prince Askery came up and informed him that he had obtained intelligence of Shyr Khān having detached Feryd Gūr in pursuit, and that the enemy were approaching. He, therefore, advised that his Majesty should immediately proceed, while he and the few remaining troops would cover his retreat. In consequence of this advice, the King mounted his horse and set off, but the followers were thrown into the greatest alarm, not knowing what to do, no one attempted to assist another, the son paid no attention to his father, nor the father to the son, but each person endeavoured to conceal whatever valuables he had, and to make his escape; to add to their distress a very heavy rain fell, in short, God preserve us from seeing such another day.

When the King found that the people were so dispirited and in such confusion, he halted, and having assembled the Princes and Nobles that were still in attendance, said to them, " formerly I had soldiers in my army from all parts of the world, some of them were killed at the battle of Chowsar, others at the battle of Canouge, those that remained are now in a wretched state; I would rather be killed myself than be the cause of such misery; I will now retreat with circumspection, and thereby hope to preserve the lives of my faithful followers;" he then ordered the troops to alight, and having divided them into three bodies, the right he gave in charge of the Prince Hindal, the left to Yadgār Myrzā, and retained the center under his own command, some other officers were appointed to bring up the rear, and the whole to march slowly and in regular array. He further ordered that if any person ventured to precede the royal division, or to plunder, he should be severely punished.

After some time a Moghul came and complained that an officer, named Chumputty Behāder, had taken his horse.

The King immediately sent a messenger with the complainant and ordered that Chumputty should give back the horse, but the insolent officer refused to do so, and made use of some improper expressions, on hearing this his Majesty commanded that he should be beheaded; the order was obeyed, the head was fixed on a spear, and shewn to the whole army, in order to frighten, render them obedient of command, and to restrain them from plundering the villages.

Marching from this place, at the rate of twenty or twenty-four miles per day, the army reached the town of Sirhind; here the Prince Hindal was ordered to remain some days, while his Majesty proceeded to Muchwāreh, situated on the banks of the Sutlege; as the river was very full and boats were scarce, it was with much delay and difficulty that the troops were carried over, in the mean time intelligence was brought that Shyr Khān had himself halted in Dehli, but that his troops were only eighty or one hundred miles in our rear.

The army having been joined soon after by Hindal's division continued its march to Jallindher, here the Prince was again ordered to halt, while the King proceeded to Lahore, and took up his abode in the house of Roushen Ayshy, on the day following he sent off Muzuffir Beg, the Turkuman, with some troops, to relieve the Prince Hindal in the defence of Jallindher, in consequence Muzuffir encamped on the western bank of the Gundwal or Beyah river, and the Afghāns soon after made their appearance on the opposite bank.

In short, his Majesty having assembled all the Princes and Nobles in Lahore, consulted with them what in this exigency was proper to be done.

In the mean time news was brought that Shyr Khān had sent an ambassador to treat of peace, the King therefore consulted with his friends, where and how he should receive the Ambassador, at length his Majesty gave orders that the interview should take place in the garden of the Prince Kamrān, and directed that all the principal inhabitants of the city from seven to seventy years of age* should attend the ceremony.

The Ambassador was accordingly admitted, and brought a letter from his master to the Prince Kamrān, who, previously to the King's arrival, had entered into a correspondence with Shyr Khān on the subject of peace, but as Shyr Khān declined entering into any treaty with him, the ambassador was dismissed. After this event the King remained inactive in the palace of Lahore not knowing what to do, or where to go; during this time he was advised by his Council to make away, in the first place, with the Prince Kamrān, whom they suspected of intriguing with the troops in order to depose his Majesty, but the King said, "No, never, for the vanities of this perishable world, will I imbrue my hands in the blood of a brother, but will for ever remember the dying words of our respected parent (Baber), who said to me, 'O Humāyūn beware, beware, do not quarrel with your brothers, nor ever form any evil intentions towards them,' these words are engraved on my heart for ever."

CHAPTER VII.

The King permits his brother Kamrān to proceed to Kabul, and his Majesty marches to Ouch, A. H. 947. A. D. 1540.

Some days after this conversation, the Prince Kamrān requested permission to wait on his Majesty, but the counsellors seeing that the Prince's followers were all armed, advised the King to have his guards on the alert and take the necessary precautions, but the King said, "there is no necessity."

* This is a general expression for young and old.

After the Prince had been seated a short time, he said to his Majesty, "Sire, since the day that your slave entered Hindūstān, he has been uneasy; there has been constantly some unfortunate circumstance occurring, and my followers are all in a wretched plight: permit me to proceed to Kabul,* where I may arrange my affairs, recruit my army, and then return to your presence." The King readily assented, and gave him his blessing.

His Majesty having at length determined on going to Moultan, the whole army having crossed the river Ravy, proceeded towards the village of Hezareh, and after a march of eight miles halted. Here his Majesty learned that the Princes Hindal and Yadgār, having been persuaded by some evil counsellors to go to Gujerāt, had quitted the army and had been followed by a number of the royal attendants.

About this time a letter was received from Kelān Beg, who commanded the district of Behēra, inviting his Majesty to come thither, and assuring him of every aid and attention in his power. Unfortunately a similar invitation was sent to the Prince Kamrān. The King not knowing this circumstance readily accepted the invitation, and proceeded towards Behēra. At the time of afternoon prayer the royal party came to the river (Chunāb), and his Majesty commanded Terdy Beg to swim his horse over as an example to the followers; but the horse after swimming a short distance turned back; on which the King ordered an elephant to be swam across; and as soon as the elephant had entered the river he spurred on his own horse, and was followed by all the party, now reduced to forty persons. They travelled all that night, and in the morning arrived at the town of Behēra.†

On his Majesty's entering the place he found that the Prince Kamrān not only had anticipated him, but had seized on the house and person of Kelān Beg. On this unlooked for intrusion his Majesty's servants were much vexed, and one of them, named Kūly Kurchy, offered to go and assassinate the Prince; but the King forbade him, and said, "I refused this request when at Lahore, and certainly will not now agree to it: go and get me a

* Kabul was long the capital and favourite residence of the Emperor Baber. See Edinburgh Gazetteer.

† Both Behēra and Khooshab are marked in the maps.

fresh horse, and I will proceed to Khushāb, and there visit Hussyn Sultān" (the ruler of that district).

The horse having been procured his Majesty continued his journey, and arrived at Khushāb the next day about noon. Here he was most hospitably received by Hussyn and his sons.

In the course of conversation the King asked him, "Host, in case of Kamrān's attempting to do with you, as he did with Kelān Beg, how would *you* act?" He replied, "I am your Majesty's attached servant, and will shed my blood in your defence." Upon this the King asked him to join the royal party, which he did.

The next day they quitted Khushāb, and proceeded towards Moultan. When they had marched twelve miles they came to a place where the road was very narrow; a little beyond this pass there are two roads; one leading to Kabul, the other to Moultan. Unluckily the royal party and the followers of Kamrān came to the pass at the same time: his Majesty wished to go through first, but Kamrān refused to give way, and said, "he would go first." The King was much displeased; on seeing which a very brave officer, named Myrzā Abū Beka, rode up to the Prince, and pointed out the impropriety of his conduct in such language that convinced him of his error; and his Majesty, having by these means cleared the pass, took the road to Moultan, and the Prince took the road leading to Kabul.

After some days his Majesty arrived at Gul Baluch, and halted. Here he was informed that the Princes Hindal and Yadgār, who had also quitted the army, had been intercepted by the Buluchians, who would not permit them to pass on to Gujerāt. At this place intelligence was also received that Khuās Khān, the Afghān general, was still in pursuit, and had arrived within forty miles of us; but this was either a false report, or he did not persevere in following us.

The Prince Hindal, Yadgār, &c. on finding they could not proceed on their journey, made a virtue of necessity, returned to the royal camp, and had the honour of kissing his Majesty's feet.

From Khushāb the royal party proceeded by easy marches to the vicinity of Ouch,* where they encamped; from this place a messenger was despatched

* The Oxydracæ of the Greeks.

to *Bukhshū Lengāh,* a powerful Zemindar, with a Firman promoting him to the title of Khān Jehān (Lord of the world); also conveying to him a banner (Tūgh), a shield, and four elephants; in return for which honour he was commanded to send provisions to the camp, and to furnish proper boats to convey the heavy baggage.* The said Bukhshū did not wait on his Majesty, but he sent the boats, &c. &c.

CHAPTER VIII.

His Majesty proceeds from Ouch to Bhiker. A. H. 948.—A. D. 1541.

As soon as Bukhshū Lengāh had sent the boats, the royal party crossed the river in the vicinity of Ouch; and marching along the banks, at length arrived at Bhiker (Baker of the maps), and alighted in the gardens of Shāh Hussyn Sultān, Ruler of Tatta,† who had assumed the title of Majesty, being lineally descended from the Emperor Timūr.

After some days the King ordered the Prince Hindal to proceed with his followers to the town of *Pāt,* which was in the district of Sehwān (Sewastan), and Myrzā Yadgār with his followers to go to Behylē, which is forty miles down the river; he also despatched Keber Beg and the Reverend (Pyr Zadē) Myr Zahir as his ambassadors to Shāh Hussyn at Tatta.

The ambassadors safely arrived at Tatta; but as a long time elapsed before any intelligence was received from them, his Majesty sent them an order either to return, or send him some information of their proceedings: they in consequence sent a letter, requesting his Majesty to have patience, and that they would shortly return. A considerable time however having passed without their coming, the King sent another order, "that if they could not prevail on Shāh Hussyn to come and pay his respects, they should instantly return to him at Bhiker."

On receipt of this order Keber Beg quitted Tatta, but left his companion to negociate the business; he however brought with him some trifling presents from Shāh Hussyn, viz. some tents and carpets, also nine horses, a camel, and a mule.

* Vessels of 200 tons may ascend the river Indus 760 miles. See Edinburgh Gazetteer.

† The Pattala of the Greeks.

After informing the King of what he had seen at Tatta, Keber Beg advised his Majesty to proceed on his journey without delay, as it was uncertain whether it was now the intention of Shāh Hussyn to wait on him, although at first he had agreed to do so; but had since altered his mind, under the pretence that the distance was too great for him to travel, and would delay his Majesty unnecessarily.

Previous to this intelligence the Prince Hindal had requested his Majesty's permission to take possession of the district of Sehwān, in the royal name; but the King forbade him, saying, "that as he had sent ambassadors to Shāh Hussyn, the Ruler of the country, he must wait their return." But as soon as the ambassador had made his report, the King communicated the subject of it to the Prince, and informed him that the royal division would soon join, and that they might then act in concert.

Accordingly the King recommenced his march, and in four days reached Behylē, where Yadgār Myrzā was encamped: the Myrzā came out to meet him, and had the honour of paying his respects.

The next day the King halted, and was most hospitably entertained by the Myrzā Yadgār. The day following the King marched on, but ordered the Myrzā to remain where he was, while he went on to join the Prince Hindal, and that he would send orders for his future proceedings.

In three days the King reached *Pāt*, which is situated twenty miles west of the Indus: the Prince Hindal came out to meet him, carried him to his own habitation, and performed all the rights of hospitality in the most affectionate and liberal manner.

CHAPTER IX.

Account of His Majesty's marriage with the ornament of women, a second Mary, Hemyd Banū Begum, and his return to Ouch. A. H. 948.—A. D. 1541.

During the King's residence at Pāt, Dildār Begum, the *mother of the Prince Hindal*, gave a grand entertainment, at which all the ladies* of the

* The Moghul Emperors were in the habit of giving entertainments to the ladies of the court, and on such occasions saw the females of all the nobility. The Virgin Mary is held in the highest respect by the Mussulmāns.

court were present; amongst these was the daughter of the Prince's preceptor, named Hemyd Banū. The King was much pleased with her, and inquired if she was betrothed. He was informed that she had been asked, but that the ceremony had not taken place: the King said, "I will marry her." On hearing this, the Prince Hindal was very angry with his brother, and said, "I thought you came here to do me honour, not to look out for a young bride: if you commit this (ridiculous) action, I will leave you."*

Dildār Begum was very angry with her son, and said, "you are speaking very improperly to his Majesty, whom you ought to consider as the representative of your late father." The Prince however would not retract; on which the King was much displeased, left the house, and went on board a boat: the mother of the Prince however followed his Majesty, brought him back to her house, made up the quarrel between him and her son, and the next day gave a nuptial banquet; after which she delivered the young lady to his Majesty, and gave them her blessing.

The royal pair marched from Pāt, and having embarked in a boat proceeded towards Bhiker. At the same time the Prince Hindal marched in an angry mood with his followers towards Candahar.

On the King's return to Bhiker he alighted in the garden where he had before resided; but after a few days he again marched towards the fort of Sehwān, leaving Myrzā Yadgār in charge of the town of Bhiker. On his Majesty's arrival at Sehwān, the governor of the fort on the part of Shāh Hussyn made a sally on the royal troops; but the officers having agreed among themselves merely to stand on the defensive until the garrison should return to the fort, when they would attempt to take it by surprise, they persuaded the King to remain quiet, and let them try the result.

As soon as night approached the governor, named Myr Alkum, returned to the fort, and took all the requisite precautions. On being thus disappointed, the royal Chiefs were ashamed of their conduct; his Majesty, there-

* Humāyūn and Hindal were by different mothers: the King was at this time 33 years of age, and Hindal only 22. As the young lady was about 14, it is probable the latter wished to marry her himself; the circumstance, although apparently trifling, was of great consequence, as it caused a feud between the brothers, and the bride subsequently became the mother of the celebrated Emperor Akber.

fore, gave orders that they should lay siege to the place, and erect batteries all around it; but Shāh Hussyn having bribed the Chiefs, they would not make any exertion to take the place. At length Aly Beg Jellayr represented to the King that he had received intelligence of Shāh Hussyn having quitted Tatta with his army, and that, if his Majesty would give him five hundred horse, he would make forced marches, surprise his camp, and destroy his army, which would be of the greatest importance in the issue of the war.

Although his Majesty was well inclined to this proposal, he could not get the Chiefs to agree to it, and nothing was done.

At length the King sent orders to Myrzā Yadgār, whom he had left at Bhiker, to send a portion of his troops to assist in taking the fort. In obedience of these orders Terdy Beg, with one hundred and fifty cavalry, joined the royal division; but even with their assistance nothing could be effected against Sehwān.

In consequence of these repeated disappointments, the Chiefs persuaded the King to raise the siege, and proceed to the northward; but the fact was that Shāh Hussyn, having embarked part of his troops on board boats, was coming up the river (Sinde) under full sail.

At this time there were several malignant reports in circulation over the country: first, that his Majesty had been thrown from his horse, and had severely bruised both his leg and his arm; second, that the troops of Shāh Hussyn had seized all the boats conveying his Majesty's stores, and that some of the women who were on board had fled half naked, and joined the camp; third, that the ambassador sent by Shāh Hussyn to make peace had been plundered on the route to the royal camp.

In consequence of the latter report, his Majesty sent Monaim Beg with a message to Shāh Hussyn to explain the circumstances, and to request that he would evince some sympathy for his sovereign in distress, and not pursue his vengeance any further; but Hussyn refused to see the messenger, and wrote an uncivil letter, asking "what benefits the King had ever conferred on him, that he should now have any consideration for his distress?"* In short, by the time that the King reached the vicinity of Bhiker the greater number of his followers had dispersed and deserted.

* His father Myrzā Shāh Arghum had been dispossessed of Candahar by the Emperor Baber.

The few remaining Chiefs then represented to his Majesty, that having safely crossed the large river Sinde, they had now no further fears of the Afghāns; it would therefore be advisable to proceed to Candahar.

The King was displeased at this advice, and said that, "never unless in a case of the greatest necessity would he take refuge, or even enter the territories of his ungrateful brothers."* He then commanded Rūshen Beg, his foster brother, to take a party with him, and collect from the villages a number of cows and buffaloes, and with their skins prepare vessels for recrossing the river. These orders were punctually obeyed; but by this time the fleet of Myrzā Hussyn was fast approaching.

When the royal party began to cross over on the skins and rafts, there was one boat remaining at the ferry, which Terdy Beg (formerly mentioned) took possession of for his own family; but the *Akā* (superintendant) of the King's household in an authoritative manner demanded it from him, saying, "empty that boat, that I may take his Majesty and the royal family over first, and then you may have it." Terdy Beg called him a scoundrel; on which the Akā replied, "he is a scoundrel who dares to act in this insolent manner." Terdy Beg, on hearing this speech, raised his horsewhip and struck the Akā: the latter instantly drew his sword, and made a blow at him, which fortunately fell on the pommel of his saddle: on seeing this the attendants separated them.

As soon as the King was informed of this distressing dispute, Terdy Beg being an officer of high rank, in order to pacify him his Majesty commanded that the hands of the Akā should be tied with a handkerchief, and led in that manner to the chief. When Terdy Beg saw this proof of the King's attention he immediately loosed the handkerchief, seated the Akā in a very polite and respectful manner, presented him with a dress and a horse, and apologised to him for his conduct.

I must now return to relate the conduct of Myrzā Yadgār.† It has been before stated that Myrzā Yadgār had been left in charge of the town of

* Kamrān had taken possession of Kabul, and Hindal had been hospitably received by the governor of Candahar.

† He was married to a daughter of the late Emperor Baber, but in consequence of his treason was finally put to death.

Bhiker, and it appears that while there, he had carried on a private correspondence with Shāh Hussyn of Tatta, who had promised him his daughter in marriage, and to confirm him as Governor of Bhiker.

In fact when the King returned to Bhiker, he observed something in the conduct of Yadgār, which raised his suspicions; but while he halted there, the Myrzā invited him to an entertainment, which he gave at a college in the vicinity of the town; and while they were seated together under a porch, which looked on the walls of the fort, the King, in order to try the effect of his guns, ordered one of them to be fired against a bastion of the fort; the shot however passed into the arsenal, and caused much confusion: in a very short time a shot was unexpectedly returned from the fort, which struck the porch under which the King was seated.

On which the King got up and went to another place; but the Myrzā said, " it was only a frolic, and that his Majesty first began it." Soon after this a person whispered to the King, " that he feared some treachery;" on which the King, having eaten very sparingly, ordered the repast to be taken off, arose and took his leave. Previously however to his Majesty's departure, the Myrzā presented him with a handsome horse, having a bridle and saddle mounted with silver, and a riding elephant, with which the King returned to his own abode.

A curious circumstance occurred shortly after, viz. one of the royal attendants, named Khuaje Muazim, took the liberty of asking the King to give him the horse presented by the Myrzā, and (as it was probably of no great value) the King gave it to him. The fellow however immediately rode it off to the Myrzā's quarters, and there offered his service as a cavalier; but the Myrzā was very angry, ordered the horse to be taken from him, and a pony to be given in exchange: he then sent the horse back to the King.

Sometime after this event the Myrzā's intentions became manifest, for he sent persons to entice the King's followers to desert to him, and even made use of severe threats to those who refused to abandon their unfortunate master.

In consequence of this insidious conduct most of the remaining chiefs meditated to desert, and his Majesty was obliged to sit up all night, and by keeping them with him prevent their going off. In the morning, the King being necessitated to go out of the tent, said to Terdy Beg and Munaim, "remain here till I return;" but as soon as he went out, they both ran towards their horses; on which one of the attendants informed his Majesty that the two chiefs were going. He desired the attendant to call them back; but as they paid no attention to the call, the King himself ran after them, and with great difficulty prevailed on them to return. After this unworthy attempt, the King ordered that Munaim should be confined, and Terdy Beg being frightened, consented to remain.

We then marched on, and arrived at a village of the district of Bhiker called *Arū*, which was a great depot of the caravans, and to which place quantities of grain and various articles were brought from Jesselmere and other towns. But as soon as the persons in charge of the caravans heard of his Majesty's approach, they began to load their camels and run off; however, a quantity of grain and other provisions were seized by the royal followers, which enabled them to halt there for some days in great abundance.

From thence we marched towards Ouch, but suffered great hardships on the route, till we reached the village of Mow, which is the boundary of the Bhiker district. After leaving Mow we met with great difficulties, especially the want of water. On one occasion his Majesty's water bottle *(Keruty)* was empty; he therefore asked his humble servant *Jouher Aftabchy* "if he had any water in the *Ewer?*" his humble servant replied, "there was water;" the King said, "pour it into the bottle." Although the water I had was for purification, I poured it into the bottle, and said, "what a horrid country this is where one cannot procure water! and as we are now travelling at night, should I be separated from your Majesty, I shall perish for want of something to drink." I then poured a small quantity of the water back into the *Ewer;* the King approved, and said, "that will be sufficient for you."

In the morning we fortunately came to a small lake, and encamped. It so happened that I was standing near the water when a deer was roused from the *Jungel*, and ran through the camp. Although many persons struck at it, it passed them and entered the lake. As soon as his Majesty was told of the circumstance he mounted his horse, with an intention of pursuing the animal, and said, "what a delicious prize this deer would be!" Seeing me, he desired I would call to a person who was standing on the other side of the lake to drive the animal back again: he did so; and as the deer was swimming, I ran into the water and endeavoured to lay hold of him, at the same time saying, "one quarter is mine;" the King replied, "very well:" luckily the animal was much tired by swimming, and I had strength enough to hold it till one of the attendants came to my assistance, and by his Majesty's orders cut its throat: when it was brought on shore the King ordered that one quarter should be given to me, two quarters were sent to the royal kitchen, and the remaining quarter to the female apartments.

At this time the mother of the future Emperor, Akber, was seven months gone with child; we therefore continued our march towards Ouch,* where after several days journey we safely arrived. From this place orders were sent to *Bukhshuy Lengah*, the Zemindar of the district, either to wait on his Majesty, or to send provisions for the royal party; but the wretch would not do one or other; nay, he even opposed the people who were sent out to purchase them, and the troops were obliged to take by force whatever was requisite for their subsistence, and, we were so much distressed that we eat the seeds and fruit or berries of trees which grew in the neighbouring jungle.

CHAPTER X.

Of his Majesty's marching again from Ouch, and of the difficulties he experienced in the Desert. A. H. 948.—A. D. 1541.

When the seeds and fruit of the trees *Sunker* and *Perhem* (probably the Jack fruit and wild bean) were all expended, it so happened that an erratic Dervish, who had been wandering through the Desert, saw a fort on the boundaries of Joudpūr, the territory of the *Rajah Maldeo*. The aforesaid Dervish immediately returned and informed his Majesty of the circumstance, who instantly said he would proceed thither. We therefore marched to the neighbourhood of the fort, and happily procured abundance of grain and water. We halted there for three days, during which time one of the officers, named Shykh Aly, proposed to the King to take possession of the

* Ouch is situated a little to the north of the 30th degree, Longitude 70,50, between the Setlege and the Indus: it is celebrated as containing the tomb of a Muhammedan saint, called Jellal addyn, and is tributary to the Ameers of Sind. See Edinburgh Gazetteer.

place by surprise; but his Majesty said, "if you could make me King of the whole world, I would not attempt so foul an action, or be guilty of such ingratitude."

In short having marched from this fort we travelled all night, and till twelve o'clock next day in the Desert, without finding water; at length we discovered some wells, and halted there.

The next day we marched at noon, and travelled for twenty-seven astronomical hours before we again found water: during this horrid journey many of our people died, and all suffered exceedingly. When about four hours of the day remained we came to a few trees, where, through the grace of God, we found a well, a rivulet, and a pond of water: here his Majesty alighted, and having prostrated himself on the ground, returned thanks to the Almighty for his beneficence. He then ordered all the water bags to be filled, to be loaded on his own horses, and to be sent back to the people who had fallen in the rear to assist them in joining the party.

It so happened that a Moghul merchant, to whom the King was much indebted, was one of the persons who from fatigue and thirst had fallen down on the road, and his son was standing by him; as the King had also rode back part of the way, he came to where the Moghul was lying, and deeming it a favourable opportunity to cancel his debt, proposed to the unfortunate sufferer, that he should have as much water as he could drink, provided he would relinquish his pecuniary demand. The poor man said, "a cup of water is, in my present situation, more valuable than the wealth of the whole world, and I consent." Three of the attendants having witnessed the agreement, the King ordered them to give him as much water as he wished: the Moghul being satiated, proceeded and joined the camp. His Majesty then gave orders to bury all the persons who had died from thirst, and to supply the survivors with abundance of water, to enable them to join the camp.

After being well recruited, we marched from the trees, and arrived at a village called *Pylpūr*; thence we proceeded to *Pehlūdy*,* where we procured abundance of grain; from thence in one march we arrived in the vicinity of the residence of the Rajā Maldeo.

* Said to lie sixty miles west of Joudpūr.

As soon as his Majesty had alighted, he sent a *Firman* to the Rajā to wait on him, but that chief made some idle excuse: he, however, sent a present of fruit.

We remained there for three days without any act of hospitality being shewn us, or any comfort given to the distressed monarch; during this time one of the King's porters, named Rajū, deserted, and informed Maldeo that the King had a number of valuable rubies and pearls in his possession; another of the royal attendants, named Muhammed Ayshek, also deserted, and instigated the Rajā to demand these jewels. When the King found that Maldeo had no intention of waiting on him, but was rather inclined to molest him, he again marched, and halted at the pond of Jougy.

CHAPTER XI.

His Majesty proceeds to Amerkote,* and the circumstances which occurred on the journey. A. H. 949.—A. D. 1542.

When his Majesty had obtained a hint of the intentions of Maldeo, he resolved to set out for Amerkote; he, therefore, ordered two of the officers to go on and seize some guides; they did so, and brought in two camel drivers. The King ordered their animals to be tied with the royal camels, and the men to be disarmed and confined: he also sent to them the Kāzy Mehdy Aly to explain, that no injury was intended them; but that if they would shew the route to Amerkote, they should be well rewarded: the two rustics pretended they knew nothing about the road, and would give no information. Some time after, they drew their daggers and killed one of the attendants who was sentinel over them; they then proceeded to where their camels were tied, stabbed them, and also a favourite horse and mule belonging to his Majesty, which reduced the royal stud to two horses and one mule. When the servants saw this, they rushed on the villagers and cut them to pieces.

This event, and other unfortunate circumstances, caused great dismay among the followers, and several of them talked of quitting his Majesty,

* It is a fortress, 30 miles east of the Indus, in the Desert. See Edinburgh Gazetteer.

who said to them, "if you leave me, whither will you go? you have now no other refuge." Notwithstanding this, Khoja Kebyr, and two others of the most confidential attendants deserted, and went to Maldeo. In this scene of distress the King determined on marching to the westward, and ordered that some of the chiefs should move on in front, and that he would follow them at a short distance with the females and servants. In this manner we proceeded till morning; but at the dawn of day we discovered three parties pursuing us, each of these parties might consist of five hundred cavalry; and to add to our consternation, we at this time had lost sight of our advanced division.

The King then enquired of some of the attendants whether they thought our pursuers were friends or enemies; and when it was agreed that they were the latter, he ordered all the baggage to be taken off the horses and placed on the camels, and that the foot soldiers should mount the horses; by these means we mustered in all sixteen troopers. His Majesty then consulted with Shykh Aly Beg, what was advisable to be done: the Shykh replied, "we are now just in the situation of the martyr Imam Hussyn:* nothing remains but to sell our lives as dearly as possible. Pardon me all the offences I have committed against you, and give me a few men with me, that I may go and bring you an account of these people." His Majesty pronounced the form of forgiveness, gave him his blessing, and sent seven horsemen with him.

The Shykh then said to his companions, "we are but few, and our enemies many; let us act separately, and when we approach them discharge our arrows simultaneously on their line, and let us trust in Providence for the consequences." The men did so, and when near the enemy let fly their arrows; and as "the decree of God is all powerful," two of their chiefs were mortally wounded, and fell from their horses; on seeing which the others all fled, and left the field to the victors. Shykh Aly then caused the two heads to be struck off, and sent them by a *Chobdar* (wand bearer) with hearty congratulations to his Majesty. When the King saw a horseman approaching, he asked his people if they knew who it was; they replied, "it is *Bhe-*

* He was the son of Aly, and grandson of the Prophet. He was murdered on his way from Mecca to Cufa, A. D. 679.

*bud** the Chobdar." The man then rode up, and having untied the heads from his saddle bow, presented them to the King, who considered the circumstance as a fortunate omen.

The King then recalled Shykh Aly, and consulted with him what was further requisite to be done; the Shykh said, " if your Majesty will be pleased to move on a short distance in front, I with my seven horsemen will protect the rear." This was agreed to, and we marched on.

I omitted to mention that, on our entering the Jesselmere district, his Majesty had detached a small party to collect provisions and bring them to the camp. It appeared that these people, having collected several cows and buffaloes, lost their way, and not knowing where to find the camp, had halted and refreshed themselves at a pond in the Desert; in this situation we fortunately found them; and their officers had again the honour of paying their respects to the King. When they heard of our miraculous escape, they were profuse in their excuses for having been absent at such a critical time, and hoped that the shadow of his Majesty would be for ever suspended over their heads, in the name of the Prophet and of his illustrious descendants.

At this place two messengers arrived from Maldeo, the Rajā of Joudpūr, who stated, " that the King had entered his territory without any invitation; and although it must be known that the killing of kine was forbidden in Hindū districts, we had nevertheless killed a number of these sacred animals; that the King having intruded himself into these parts, he was now completely in the Rajā's power, and must take the consequences."

His Majesty consulted his friends what answer he should give to this message; they replied, " that as there was no chance of coming to an amicable arrangement, the only mode was to put a bold face on the matter and confine the messengers." This was done, and we marched on; but on passing one of the forts of Jesselmere, the garrison came out and attacked us: the skirmish lasted for several hours; during which time they severely wounded several of our people; at length they returned to their fort. At the distance of ten miles from this spot, we came to a village where we found plenty of grain and water, but no vestige of any human being.

* Signifies, Good Luck, &c.

About this period the Rajā ordered his son, who was also named Maldeo, to precede our march, and to fill up all the wells with sand, so that we might perish for want of water. The son obeyed these orders; so that after we left the above mentioned village, and had arrived at the next stage, we found all the wells choked up with sand: we were therefore compelled to proceed on a second stage. Here we experienced the same difficulty; but as we were too much fatigued to proceed further, we were obliged to halt there during the night.

On this occasion the King ordered the camels to be placed in a circle round the horses and tents, directed that the people should be on the alert, and said, "he would himself keep watch by walking round the circle all night." Shykh Aly would not consent to this proposal; but insisted on his Majesty's lying down, and that he himself should keep watch. On this the King went and lay down; whilst he was asleep, a thief came into the camp, took the sword from under his Majesty's head, and drew it half out; but being alarmed, left it in that situation and went away.

When the King awoke, he saw that his sword was half way drawn from the scabbard, and was much astonished; he therefore called to the servant, who was sleeping at the foot of the bed, and asked him if he had drawn the sword; who replied, "that he would not have ventured to do so for the world."

In short we marched from that place, and arrived at a stage where there were four wells, in three of which we found water, but the fourth was choked up. In order to secure an equal division of the water, his Majesty assigned one of the wells for his own household; the second he gave to Terdy Beg and his followers, and the third to Khaled Beg and attendants; as we had no buckets to draw the water, a copper pot was let down, and pulled up by a camel; but as the well was very deep, and the pot a long time coming up, in order to prevent the people from crowding round the mouth of the well, they were directed to keep at a distance till a *drum* was beaten to give notice of the proper time, when they should be regularly served in turn: notwithstanding this precaution, in consequence of the anxiety to be first served, much quarrelling took place among the people; at length the domestics of his Majesty came and complained that Terdy Beg had given water to his own horses and camels, but would not let them have any for their animals; they also swore, that if he did not supply them they would fight for it, and either have water, or be killed. On this his Majesty, fearing contention, rode to the well, and said to Terdy Beg in the *Tūrky language*, "be so good as draw off your people for a short time from the well till mine are served, which will prevent disputes." Terdy Beg complied with his Majesty's command, and the servants procured a scanty supply of water; in short the misery we suffered at this stage was intolerable.*

About this time the son of the Rajā of Joudpūr, having in his hand a white flag, came in sight of our party, and sent a messenger to request an audience of his Majesty; the man having been admitted, delivered the following message: "You have entered this country without any invitation; and "although you well knew that in all Hindū countries it is forbidden to kill "kine, your people have frequently done so; if you had acted with due "politeness, you should have informed me of your wishes to pass through "my country; I should then have performed the rights of hospitality towards "you, as is the custom of all Hindū princes, or Zemindars. Now, if you "choose to halt here for some time, I will send bullocks to draw the water, "and will give you some buckets; but it was very unkind and improper in you "to confine my two messengers; I therefore desire you will release them."

After some consultation the King ordered the two messengers to be released; and having learned that at the next stage there was only one well, he gave orders that we should move in three divisions, at a day's interval; the first party to consist of the royal family, escorted by Terdy Beg; the second party to be under the command of Munaim Beg, and the third under charge of Shykh Aly: notwithstanding this precaution, a number of people died on this journey through thirst.

At length we arrived within twenty miles of the fort of Amerkote; but here a very distressing circumstance occurred, viz. the horse of an officer, named Rūshen Beg, having been knocked up, he insisted on taking one which he had lent the Queen; when his Majesty was informed of this transaction, he immediately alighted from his horse, sent it to the Queen, and, after walking some distance, mounted a camel belonging to the *Ewer* department; in this manner we proceeded three or four miles; when Khaled

* See Dow's Hindūstān, vol. ii. page 156.

Beg rode up and presented his horse to his Majesty. Some hours after this the King entered Amerkote, attended by only seven horsemen. The Ranā Pursaud sent his brother to wait on his Majesty with a polite message, "that the day was not a fortunate one, but hoped that on the following day "he would mount the throne." Provisions were then supplied for the whole party, all of whom joined us during the course of the day.

On the following morning the Ranā Pursaud had the honour of paying his respects, and congratulated his Majesty on his safe arrival; he then represented that he had 2000 horsemen of his own tribe, and 5000 cavalry belonging to his allies, all of whom were devoted to him with heart and soul: these troops were at his Majesty's service, and by their aid he might easily conquer the districts of Tatta and Bhiker.

The King replied, "that he had no money to pay the troops with, but probably he might raise some from his attendants." On hearing this, Shāh Muhammed whispered "that he knew where they, the servants, had hidden their valuables."

Soon after the Ranā had retired the King undressed, and ordered his clothes to be washed, and in the meanwhile he wore his dressing gown; while thus sitting, a beautiful bird flew into the tent, the doors of which were immediately closed, and the bird caught; his Majesty then took a pair of scissors and cut some of the feathers off the animal; he then sent for a painter, and had a picture taken of the bird, and afterwards ordered it to be released.

About this time the King ordered all the officers to assemble in the tent, and while they were there seated, he sent some of his confidential domestics under the direction of Shāh Muhammed to search the baggage of the officers, and to bring to him whatever valuables or money they might find. The servants went, and having examined all the portmanteaus and bags, and opened the camel saddles, found some money and other valuables, which they laid down before his Majesty. It happened that an old woman, having a small box, gave it in charge of Hussyn Kurchy to take care of till we should arrive in a place of safety; on seeing what was going forward, Hussyn endeavoured to conceal the box, but he was seized with it in his hands, and brought before the King. When the box was opened, it was found to contain three (Bricks) ingots of pure gold, forty-two gold Mohrs, and several golden and inlaid trinkets. Kafūr, one of the eunuchs, was ordered to cut the end of Hussyn's ear as a punishment for his treachery, but the eunuch mistaking the order, cut off the *whole* ear; on seeing this the King was very angry, sent for a surgeon, and had the ear sewn on again, assisted in the operation, and apologized to the sufferer. When all the plunder was collected, his Majesty ordered that one half of the money should be restored to the owners, the other half to be divided among the servants and followers; but of the clothes he took one half for his own use, and the other half he gave back to the proprietors.

After some time his Majesty again consulted the Ranā on what was most advisable to be done. The Ranā advised that the King should proceed to Tatta,* or go on to *Jūn*, where he might depend upon being joined by all the people of that district. Having adopted this advice, his Majesty waited for a fortunate hour, and then commenced his journey, leaving all his family in the fortress of Amerkote: the first day we marched twenty-four miles, and encamped on the banks of a large pond.

CHAPTER XII.

Birth of the Prince Muhammed Akber, may God perpetuate his kingdom, in the fortress of Amerkote—and the events that followed. A. H. 949—A. D. 1542.

The next day, while the King was encamped at the large pond, a messenger arrived from Amerkote with the joyful intelligence of the birth of a son and heir. This auspicious event happened on the night of the full moon of the month Shābān 949; in consequence of which his Majesty was pleased to name the child, The Full Moon of Religion (Budr addyn) Muhammed Akber. On this joyful occasion he prostrated himself, and returned thanks to the Almighty Disposer of all events.†

When this joyful news was made known, all the chiefs came and offered

* The capital of the Delta of the Indus. See Edinburgh Gazetteer.

† As the mother of Akber was the young lady the King married in the IXth Chapter, he must have spent nearly a year in the vicinity of the Indus. The Author has here probably made a mistake, the birth took place in the month of Rejub, and the title was Jellal addyn, Glory of religion. See Price's Muhammedan History, vol. iii. page 807.

their congratulations. The King then ordered the author of this memoir (Jouher) to bring him the articles he had given in trust to him; on which I went and brought two hundred *Shāhrūkhys* (silver coin), a silver bracelet, and a pod of musk; the two former he ordered me to give back to the owners from whom they had been taken, as formerly mentioned; he then called for a China plate, and having broken the pod of *musk*, distributed it among all the principal persons, saying, "this is all the present I can afford to make you on the birth of my son, whose fame will I trust be one day expanded all over the world, as the perfume of the *musk* now fills this apartment." After this ceremony the drums were beaten, and the trumpets proclaimed the auspicious event to the world.

As soon as the evening prayers were finished we marched from the pond, attended by a number of the Amerkote Ranā's troops, and one hundred Moghuls, commanded by Shykh Aly Beg. After five marches we arrived in the vicinity of *Jūn;** here we found Jany Beg, the former possessor of Amerkote and a celebrated *Cossac*, drawn up with a formidable body of his cavalry to oppose us. The Jāt troops of the Ranā and the Moghuls immediately charged the Cossacs, put them to flight, and killed a number of them; amongst the prisoners taken was a Moghul deserter, who had been severely wounded in the face. On being brought before the King, Myrzā Kūly said in the Tūrky language, "this is the fellow that abused your Majesty on such an occasion;" the King said, "well, he has received his reward, let him go:" but he ordered all the other prisoners to be killed.

After this affray we moved on, and took possession of Jūn, where the royal tent was pitched in a large garden. At this place a number of Zemindars came and offered their services to the King, who first employed them to dig a deep ditch all round the garden, so as to form it into a respectable fort; from this place a messenger was despatched to Amerkote to bring the young Prince and his mother. On the 20th of the month of Ramzān the Prince arrived, and had the honour of being first embraced by his Majesty on the 35th day of his age.†

* See note at the end of Part I.

† As this circumstance corroborates the date before mentioned, it is *possible* that Abul Fazil may have made a mistake in the Akber Nameh, though not likely.

I am now obliged to revert to some circumstances which occurred in the last year, in order to preserve my narrative. During the period that the King laid siege to Sehwān, it was observed that a soldier in the fort made so good a use of his musquet, that he never failed to hit some of our people; on which his Majesty said, "I hope I shall one day get hold of that fellow;" he also said, "I wish I could catch the person who took the sword from under my head, and drew it half way out of the scabbard." By chance it now happened that these two men were both in *Jūn* when we took it; and having met in an arrack shop were boasting of their feats of bravery: their conversation having been overheard, they were seized and brought before the King, who, after inquiry, ordered the musqueteer to be put to death, but forgave the thief, and made him a handsome present.

During our stay at Jūn the King issued orders that all the Chiefs of that country should wait on him; in consequence of which, the Rajās of Sudhā, of Symech, of Cutch, and Jām, who was formerly the Chief of Bhiker, had the honour of paying their respects, and not less than fifteen or sixteen thousand horsemen were collected.

About this time Shāh Hussyn having marched from Tatta, arrived within eight miles of Jūn, and took post on the bank of the river (Indus). It was one evening during the fast of Ramzān, just as his Majesty had taken his first mouthful of water, that intelligence was brought him of the desertion of Tersh Beg, and of his having joined his enemy Hussyn. This news greatly affected the King, and he said, "may a speedy death overtake him!" and it really so happened that the arrow of Fate did suddenly strike him; for when he arrived with Shāh Hussyn, the latter made him a present of a slave, who having soon after committed some fault, Tersh Beg cut his nose; in revenge for which, three days afterwards, the slave assassinated him: upon hearing this, the people all declared that "the King was a worker of miracles;" and no wonder, as it is written in the Korān, that "the Kings are the Vicegerents of God," and is a proof of the legitimacy of our monarch, the Emperor Humāyūn.

About this time, Shāh Hussyn sent from Tatta a messenger to the Ranā of Amerkote, then with the Emperor; and in order to induce the Ranā to desert to his party, sent him an honorary dress, a rich dagger, and several other presents. The Ranā immediately brought these presents, and shewed them all to the King, who desired him to put them on a dog, and send them back to his master. This was actually done; and caused Shāh Hussyn to be much ashamed of himself.

Some time after this event an unfortunate quarrel took place between one of the Moghul chiefs, named Khauajē Ghāzy, and the Ranā, who in consequence of the dispute left the camp with all his followers, saying, "that any attempt to assist the Moghuls was a loss of labour and time." As soon as the Ranā had abandoned us, all the Zemindars also returned to their own homes, and left us to our fate. The following day Munaim Beg also deserted, and informed Shāh Hussyn that the Emperor was now left alone, and was encamped on an open plain, where he might be easily seized or defeated. Luckily this conversation was reported to his Majesty, who instantly ordered all his people to set to, and dig a ditch round the encampment; he even in person took a stick in his hand and pointed out to each party where they were to commence working; and so much diligence was used, that in three days the ditch was completed; so that when Shāh Hussyn arrived and found the camp well fortified, he accused Munaim Beg of having deceived him; in short some skirmishing took place between the adverse parties, and Mahmūd Gird Bāz, one of our chiefs, was killed.

During this time intelligence was brought that Byram Beg (Khān),* who had fled from the battle of Canouge, was come from Gujerāt to join his Majesty. On hearing this joyful news the King ordered all the chiefs to go out and meet him: he was shortly introduced, and had the honour of being presented to his Majesty, who was much rejoiced by the arrival of so celebrated a character.

The following night the *Bastard*, Shāh Hussyn, came to the edge of our ramparts and blew his trumpets: on hearing them Byram Beg and several other chiefs sallied forth, but his Majesty recalled Byram, and ordered Rūshen Beg and others to pursue the fugitives: they did so; and when arrived near the enemy's camp a duel took place between Rūshen Beg and Baber Kūly, one of our opponents: Rūshen unhorsed his adversary; but a foot soldier cut the thigh of his horse in such a manner, that although he

* Afterwards preceptor and guardian of the Prince Akber. See Dow's Hindūstān.

brought his master back to the camp, he immediately died. This is said to be a peculiar quality or virtue of the *Tupchāk* horses.

After this affair his Majesty ordered Shykh Aly Beg to proceed to *Chekaw*, and from thence send grain to the camp, which he accordingly performed; but Shāh Hussyn having heard of this, sent a superior party to cut off our supplies; in consequence of which the King ordered off Tehur Sultān to reinforce our detachment: this measure however gave offence to Shykh Aly, who complained of the supercession, which caused a quarrel between these two officers.

His Majesty being now wearied of the confinement to his entrenchments, said, "that the next time Shāh Hussyn approached the camp, he would go out in person and chastise him;" and orders were given to have his arms and horses in readiness; we were therefore in expectation that a battle would take place the ensuing day, although it was in the holy month of Ramzān; but during the night a man came from the bank of the river, and said, "that some person on the opposite side was calling for a boat." The King commanded that they should inquire his name, and what he wanted with a boat; he replied, "that he was Tehur Sultān;" on hearing this his Majesty said, "God grant that all may be well!" in short a boat was sent over, and he was brought into the presence, where he reported that the convoy had been attacked, that Shykh Aly was killed, and that *he* had with difficulty made his escape.

As the King had determined to go out next morning to battle, he was much affected by this news, and did not sleep during the whole night.

In the mean time Shāh Hussyn, having received reinforcements, was also resolved upon battle; but during that night a chief, named Muhammed Bynuaz, deserted to him, and communicated the cutting off of our detachment, and of the King's intention of engaging him the next day. He added, that as his Majesty was now desperate, he advised him (Shāh Hussyn) to conciliate matters.

In consequence of this advice Shāh Hussyn, some days afterwards, sent the chief, Baber Kūly, with a few trifling presents to the King, accompanied by an apology for his past conduct, and an assurance that shame alone prevented him from paying his respects in person. His Majesty in a condescending manner asked the ambassador to tell him the circumstances of the duel between him and Rūshen Beg. He repeated that Rūshen Beg had dismounted him with his lance, but did not injure him any farther, and that some other person had wounded his competitor's horse; his Majesty then sent for Rūshen Beg, and made them embrace each other. After this his Majesty dismissed the ambassador, with an assurance that he would immediately quit the country of Sinde.

CHAPTER XIII.

His Majesty marches from Sinde, and proceeds towards Candahar. A. H. 950.—A. D. 1543.

When the ambassador, Baber Kūly, returned to his master, and informed him that the King was ready to quit the country on certain conditions, he agreed to send to his Majesty two thousand loads of grain, and three hundred camels, to be delivered at the village of *Rutay* or Runay, from which place he assured the King that he might procure all other requisites for proceeding to Candahar. In consequence of this amicable agreement, his Majesty put all his baggage on board boats, crossed the river, and halted in the village of Rutay, till the grain and camels arrived; soon after which a distribution was made of them to all the followers; after which we proceeded towards Suhān (Sehwān.)

It here becomes necessary to relate, that Yadgār Nasir Khusru Myrzā, who had been deceived by the deceitful promises of Shāh Hussyn of a kingdom, and his daughter in marriage, as formerly related, having in consequence been puffed up with pride, now suffered a severe retribution, by having been expelled by Hussyn, and obliged to pay a *Shāhrūkhy* (silver coin) for each camel, and five similar coins for every horse belonging to his followers; after which he was sent in great disgrace across the river: "may such be the reward of every person that forsakes his liege lord!"

In short, his Majesty having passed Sehwān, in two more marches reached Futtypūr Kundavy (Gundava of the maps); from thence, in two other marches, he arrived at a station situated between two ponds of water; one of which was brackish, the other sweet: at this time the King asked which was the pond of sweet water; the guide replied, "that it was the one which we had left seven *coss* in our rear." On hearing this his Majesty was much displeased, and demanded why the camp had not been pitched at the sweet water, but learned that this was a manœuvre of Shāh Hussyn's, in order to annoy us.

The King however rode back with a few of his attendants to the sweet water pond, leaving all the heavy baggage and followers at the brackish water; but as it was the first watch of the night when we reached the good water, the first thing his Majesty did was to perform his ablutions, and say his prayers; after which he and all the servants quenched their thirst; then, having rested for some time, each person took with him as much water as he could carry, and returned to the camp.

The people being much fatigued with their long march, we halted till two o'clock of the following day. When we had nearly reached the next stage, the camel which carried the purifying vessel being much tired, fell down, and could not move; on which the humble servant, *Jouher Aftabchy*, represented the circumstance to his Majesty, who gave orders that the servants should unload the camel, and bring the vessels into the camp; but no one paid any attention to these orders, and the humble servant being left nearly alone with the camel, was attacked by robbers, who wounded him with an arrow, and struck his companion with an axe. On this I bawled out to some people who were nearer the camp, "that the robbers had attacked me, and carried away all the contents of the sacks (*Suleetas*)." The people repeated my cries to those who were in the camp, and the King hearing the noise enquired what was the matter. Terdy Beg replied, "that it was only the shouts of some people who were playing;" the King said, "I hear the cry of robbers, what kind of play do you call that?" On this the chief eunuch galloped his horse to where I was, and saw that the thieves had carried away all the brazen vessels; he, therefore, took hold of the camel and led him into the camp.

The next day we again marched, and encamped in an open plain, the soil of which has two opposite effects; in the hot season the *Semum* blows with such violence, that the very limbs of a man are melted, and he dies; but in the winter the cold is so severe, that if a person takes his soup out of the pot, and pours it into a plate, it becomes instantly a piece of ice.

In short, all our people who were without warm clothing, suffered very severely; but on this occasion his Majesty, who had a fur cloak, graciously ordered it to be unlined, the exterior part of which he gave to Byram Beg, who had suffered much from the cold, and sent the lining to Mehter Anys. We again marched, and arrived at *Salmustan* or Mustung, which is one of the districts of Candahar.

In this place the King alighted in a garden; soon after which a man came up, and asked him, " if he knew any thing about Myrzā Askery?" his Majesty replied, " he did not; but if he could give any information regarding the Myrzā, he would be obliged to him:" the man whispered, " send away your servants." This was done, and I only remained. The man said, " send him off also:" the King replied, " he is only a boy; there is no fear." On which he said, " before two watches of the morning shall be passed, Myrzā Askery will be here; his object is to seize your Majesty." The King asked him from whom he had this information? the man replied, " my son is one of the Myrzā's servants, and left him in the hills about five coss from hence, but having come alone, has arrived here before him." On hearing this news the King came into the camp, and breakfasted on whatever he could get.

After dinner his Majesty said, " the people of Hindūstān have an extraordinary mode of evincing their fidelity;" then turning to the servants, he said, " don't you be afraid, if it please God all your wishes shall be accomplished." On which the servants all raised their hands in prayer for his prosperity.

The next day the King arose with the dawn, and said his prayers; after which he lay down, and fell asleep; and the servants took this opportunity of going about their own business. At mid-day a horseman came out of the jungle at full gallop, and asked where the King was; the servant said, " alight; leave your horse here, and go in." The man twisted the reins about his hand, entered the skreens where the King was lying, and awoke him. The man then asked, " have you heard any news?" the King said, " no:" the man replied, " Myrzā Askery is coming to attack you;" his

Majesty asked, " what is your name?" he said, " Juy Behadur, of the Uzbeg tribe, and am sent by Kasim Hussyn Sultān." On hearing this news the King ordered Byram Beg to be called; and when he came, consulted with him what was proper to be done.

Byram Beg advised his Majesty to move on immediately; the King said, " let us try a battle;" Byram replied, " there are but few of us, and our adversaries are very numerous; we had much better make our escape from this place;" but the King argued that he had two good blunderbusses, and most of the servants had fire arms;" he added, " at least let us fire a volley upon these scoundrels, and let us see to whom God will give the victory."

But as the Prince Askery's troops were known to be numerous, and we had but a few people, it was at length agreed to march on; his Majesty then asked Terdy Beg for the loan of his horse, but that officer refused, and the King was obliged to place the *Begum* on his own horse. The royal party was now reduced to forty-two persons, viz. forty men and two women; one of them her Majesty, Mariam Mukany; the other, the wife of Hussyn Aly, named Ayshek Akā, who was the daughter of a Bulouch chief; for his Majesty finding that it was requisite to leave the young Akber, then a year and a half old, behind, ordered all the domestics to remain with him.

Soon after the King's departure, Khuajē Sekunder, the Sudder (Justice) of Myrzā Askery, arrived in the camp, and not finding his Majesty there, said, " the object of my master's coming, was merely to pay his respects to the King, why has he ventured to enter these jungles?" After an hour or two the Myrzā also arrived; upon which, we, the servants, took up the young child, and presented it to him: the Myrzā took the babe in his arms, and embraced it. He then ordered all the effects of his Majesty to be brought before him. Amongst other things was a chest, in which were several curious stones, of an opium colour; as the chest was heavy, the Myrzā supposed that it contained money; he therefore ordered it to be opened, and finding only stones, was much mortified.

In short, the Myrzā ordered the young Prince to be carried to Candahar, and I, the author, attended the child thither; but I shortly afterwards deserted, and rejoined his Majesty in the city of Herat.

Soon after my arrival the King did me the honour to inform me, that the royal party, consisting of forty horsemen and two women, as before mentioned, having quitted the camp, travelled all night; during part of which time they heard some dogs bark; his Majesty then said, "there must be a village here;" and immediately several Bulouches came up and stopped the road. His Majesty addressed them, and asked who they were; but as they replied in a language he did not understand, he enquired of the Bulouch lady, the wife of Hussyn Aly, what they said? she interpreted, "that they were followers of Mulk Khutty; but as their chief was absent, they insisted that the King must alight, and stop till he arrived; in the mean time he might come into the fort or village, and rest himself." The King did so, and the Bulouches very politely saluted him, and spread a carpet for him to sit on. The King and the Begum sat down on the carpet, attended by the eunuch Anber. Shortly after the day broke, and his Majesty performed the morning prayer. About this time Mulk Khutty arrived; and as he was approaching, the King said to himself, "now if this person means to be friendly, he will come on my right side; but if on the left, his intentions will be the contrary."

The chief however advanced to the King's right side, and enquired after his health; he then said, "three days ago I received orders from the Myrzā Kamrān, that if your Majesty came this road, to stop and seize you; nevertheless, as your Majesty has done me the honour of coming hither, I will not obey the Prince's orders; but I request you will again mount your horse, and I will escort you safely to my boundaries." The King immediately complied with this request, and the Bulouch chief convoyed the King the distance of fifteen coss, even to the limits of his own territory, and then respectfully took his leave.

The next march brought us to the district of *Gurm Syr* (warm climate), which forms the boundary between Candahar and Khorāsān.* The stupid

* Gurmseir, a fertile district of Afghānistan, situated on both banks of the river Hermund, lying principally between the latitudes of 30 and 32 N. Gurmseir signifies "warm climate;" on which account it is applied to several other districts of Persia and Afghānistan, whither the pastoral tribes drive and keep their flocks during the winter season, at the expiration of which they again remove to the hills or mountains, called by them *Serd Seir*, Cold Climate. Edinburgh Gazetteer.

chief of that country, named Abdal Hy, paid no attention to his Majesty, but one of his servants prepared an entertainment for the King, which so incensed the chief, that he actually put out the servant's eyes.

While we were at this place, Khuajē Jellal addyn, who was one of the followers of Myrzā Askery, deserted from Candahar, and joined the King, to whom he made an offering of some tents and skreens, and several mules and horses; in reward for which his Majesty conferred on him the title of (Myr Saman) "steward of the household," for which he returned thanks.

We then moved on, and after several days entered Seistan, a province of Persia,* of which Kara Sultān Shamlū was the governor, who immediately advanced to meet his Majesty; and having paid his respects, made an offering of a celebrated horse called *Leilet al Kudder* (the night of power), after which he conducted the King to his own habitation, and performed all the rights of hospitality. He further invited the King to remain there, till he should be joined by all his followers from Candahar. The King agreed, and in a few days was joined by several chiefs.

After some days had elapsed, Byram Beg and the other chiefs represented to his Majesty, that the King of Persia might possibly take offence at our having entered his territories without due notice; it would therefore be proper to write to him for permission to proceed. A letter was in consequence written, and sent, the contents of which were, "we are arrived in your country, and await your royal orders:" the remainder of the letter was in verse, and replete with compliments.

On receipt of this letter, the Monarch of Persia, the *Asylum of the world*, issued orders to all his governors and officers to pay the King Humāyūn every attention in their power, and to conduct themselves in every respect

* Seistan, an extensive province in the east of Persia: it is 300 miles in length, and 160 in breadth. The modern capital is Dooshah, in the neighbourhood of which are immense ruins, situated in N. Lat. 31-10. The western part of Seistan consists of a vast and arid plain, intersected with one or two ranges of mountains; in the midst of which is situated the city of Kubbees. This country is now formed into a number of small independent states; Byram Khān Kyāny assumes the title of Chief of Seistan. Edinburgh Gazetteer.

In page 129 of Hanway's Travels, it is stated that Mahmūd the Afghān lost 2000 men in crossing this desert.

towards him, as they would to his Majesty himself; he also sent a consolatory letter, assuring the King of his support, and inviting him to proceed to his court.

Note.—The town of Jūn or Jown is not to be found in any of the maps I have access to, but it is mentioned in the Ayeen Akbery as being in the Sirkar Hajykan, and yielding a large revenue: it is also described by Abul Fazil as being situated on the Indus, and as a most delightful place.

The route of the King appears to have been across Buloochistan, viz. from Sehwān to Gundava; thence probably to Kelat, and Shurabek to the vicinity of Candahar, where being obliged to cross the Hiermund river, he entered Gurmsyr, and from thence by the town of Ferrah to Herat. See Map prefixed to Malcolm's History of Persia. See also Beloochistan; Edinburgh Gazetteer.

END OF PART I.

ADVERTISEMENT TO THE SECOND PART

OF THE

MEMOIRS OF THE MOGHUL EMPEROR HUMĀYŪN.

Although more has been written about Persia than of any foreign country of which we have a knowledge, the want of a concise and connected narrative of the events that have occurred there, render its *history* but very little known. The compilers of gazetteers have considered it an unfathomable ocean, and therefore have not even dipped into it. Hanway's Travels, and Sir John Malcolm's splendid History, supply ample materials; but both these books are so large and so expensive, that few people have an opportunity, or leisure, to consult them: of the latter I could not procure a single copy in the extensive city of Bath.

I have therefore thought it requisite, before Humāyūn's entering Persia, to give a *sketch* of its history, that the reader may be in some measure introduced to the people about to be described.

The conquest of Persia by Alexander the Great took place about A. M. 3635.

The nominal conquest by the Romans, under Trajan, about A. D. 100.

It was then governed by native dynasties till the year of our Lord 628, when it was subdued by the Arabians, and for about 180 years it remained subject to the Khalifs of Bagdad.

In the early part of the eighth century, the governors of the provinces assumed independence, and Persia was divided between a number of contending princes.

In the twelfth century these petty princes were all subdued by the Tartar or Tūrk Zingis (Jengyz) Khān, whose empire extended from the eastern borders of China to the shores of the Mediterranean sea. The descendants of that conqueror, although disunited among themselves, retained possession of Persia till the end of the fourteenth century, when they were all subdued by the Great Moghul, Timūr.

Some time after the death of Timūr, the Uzbegs got possession of the northern provinces of Persia. But it is related in the *Memoirs of Timūr*,* that after the defeat of Bajazet, the conqueror while returning towards his own dominions (A. D. 1402-3), in passing through the city of Ardebyl, visited a celebrated Musselmān Saint, called *Shykh Sudder addyn Seffy*, and at the termination of the interview, the Emperor asked the Saint what he could do to oblige him? the Saint replied, "liberate your captives;" the Emperor responded, "I not only liberate them, but give them to you." He did so; and these captives, amounting to 40,000 persons, many of them of good family, became the devoted adherents of the Saint, and their posterity continued the same attachment to his descendants.

This celebrated character (the Saint) claimed his descent in a direct line from Aly, the son-in-law of the Arabian prophet, and was a strenuous advocate for the rights of his progenitors, and thereby became the leader of the sect of Shyāhs in Persia. He is said to have been assassinated, but his magnificent tomb still exists at Ardebyl, and must not be confounded with the mausoleum of *Shāh* Seffy, which is at Kom; both are described in Chardin's Travels. The Saint left three grandsons, the youngest of whom, Juneyd, was brought up privately in the province of Ghilan. He was educated in the tenets of his grandfather, with an avowed enmity to the reigning powers, and was killed by the Prince of Shirwān. He was succeeded by his son Hyder, whose mother having been a daughter of Uzun Hussen, the Uzbeg Chief, found a number of adherents; but he was also killed in an attack on Shirwān.

Ismael, third son of Hyder, was a child during these events; but at the age of fourteen he put himself at the head of his followers, attacked the Ruler of Shirwān, and defeated him. Ismael then assumed the title of Shāh, and became one of the most celebrated monarchs of the age. He is said to have died A. H. 930, A. D. 1523.

He was succeeded by his eldest son Tahmāsp Myrzā, then only ten years of age, the person whose protection, nineteen years afterwards, was sought by the unfortunate Exile of Hindūstān. Authors differ much with regard to

* Published in 1831 for the Oriental Translation Fund, see page 7.

the character of this Prince; but we cannot do less than transcribe the portrait given of him by the able historian of Persia. (See Persian History, vol. i. page 508.)

"The reign of Tāmāsp owes much of its celebrity to the truly royal and "hospitable reception he gave to the Emperor Hoomāyun when that monarch "was obliged to fly from India, and to take shelter in his dominions. The "Persians have in all ages boasted of their hospitality; and the vanity of "every individual is concerned in supporting the pretensions of his country "to a superiority over others in the exercise of this national virtue. The "arrival of the fugitive Hoomāyun presented an opportunity of a very sin-"gular nature for the display of this noble quality; and we know no "example of a distressed monarch being so royally welcomed, so generously "treated, and so effectually relieved." The reader is requested to keep this panegyric in recollection.

During the greater part of Shāh Tahmāsp's reign, he was engaged in wars with Solimān the Turkish emperor. He died at the age of sixty-four,* after a reign of more than fifty-three years. The Seffy (Sophy) dynasty ruled over Persia for two centuries, which period may be considered as its Augustan age.† Their names were: Shāh Ismael Seffy.

.... Tahmāsp.
.... Ismael II.
.... Mohammed.
.... Abbas, the Great.
.... Seffy, the Cruel.
.... Abbas II.
.... Solimān.
.... Hussyn.
.... Tahmāsp II.

The Seffys were displaced by the Afghāns, who took the title of Sultān, but in their turn were expelled (A. D. 1736) by the celebrated Nadir Shāh.

The descendants of Nadir were overturned by the Zend family, who were succeeded by the Cajars (a Tūrky tribe), of whom Futteh Aly Shāh, the present monarch, is the second of that dynasty.

* See Appendix.

† See Travels by Chardin, Hanway, Morier, and Ousely; also Malcolm's History.

MEMOIRS OF HUMĀYŪN.

PART II.—CHAPTER XIV.

Arrival of Shāh Tahmāsp's letter, and the march of Humāyūn towards Meshehed. A. H. 950-1.—A. D. 1543-4.

I think it requisite to repeat, that after the King had entered the province of Khorasan, and had arrived at the city of Herat, which is the capital of that country, he was waited upon by Muhammed Khān, the preceptor (Atalyk) of the young Prince Sultān Muhammed (eighth son of Tahmāsp), who had previously given orders that every person of the city from seven years of age to seventy should advance to meet his Majesty; in consequence of which, the Prince, the preceptor, and an immense crowd of people, had the honour of paying their respects to the King, for whom an encampment was formed in the Murād Bagh (Garden of desire).

After we had remained about a month in this delightful situation, another letter arrived from the Persian monarch, inviting the King to proceed to Meshehed-Sheryf,* where he would have the honour of meeting him.

At this time Bubek Beg, one of the nobles of Aby Khān who had taken refuge with his Majesty, represented, that as it was his anxious wish to make the pilgrimage of Mecca, he requested permission to attend the royal stirrup to Arabia; but that if his Majesty should alter his intention, he might be permitted to accompany him as far as Meshehed, being assured that while under his Majesty's protection the Persian monarch would not be displeased; and that from Meshehed he would proceed on the pilgrimage by himself. To this proposal the King very good-naturedly gave his consent.†

* See Edinburgh Gazetteer.

† It was one of the King's objects in going to Persia, to proceed on the pilgrimage to Mecca, if not supported by Shāh Tahmāsp in the recovery of his dominions.

In short, after various marches we arrived safely at the Holy Meshehed;* the governor of the city, named Shāh Kūly Sultān, having come out to meet the King, had the honour of paying his respects, and performed all the rites of hospitality.

We remained forty days in that city; when one night it entered the mind of his Majesty, that he would go privately and make his prostrations at the tomb of the Imām Aly, son of Musa, on whom be the peace of God! He therefore selected five persons to attend him on this solemn occasion: their names were, Doust Baba, the Kourbegy (Chamberlain), Mehter Vasil, the Tushekbeg (Keeper of the wardrobe), Yakūb Beg, the Suferchy (Butler), Kuchekbeg, and the humble servant Jouher, the Aftabchy. When we reached the tomb, the porter attempted to open the gate, but the chain was closed; the door-keeper then represented that it was impossible to open the chain: the King in consequence retreated a few steps, but afterwards returned, and said, "O Imām, every person who has ever offered up his vows at your shrine has obtained the object of his wishes; your slave has also come with similar hopes to your tomb, in expectation of succeeding in his request." Having said this, he laid his hand on the door, when instantly the chain was unlocked; it might even be said it was cut in two: on which his Majesty entered the holy tomb, walked round it, and then offered up his prayers, after which he sat down at an appointed place, and began to read the Korān.

The superintendant of the tomb then said to the King, "if you like you may snuff the lamp;" his Majesty replied, "if not too great a liberty, I will do so;" the officer said, "you have leave."† The King therefore took up the scissors, and cut off the snuff of the lamp; after which having said his prayers, he came out, but commanded that one of the royal bows should be suspended on the gate as an offering.

Soon after this event another letter arrived from the sovereign of Persia,

* It was formerly called Tūs, and contains the tomb of the eighth Imām, Aly, the son of Musa, who was held in the highest respect by the Persians, and pilgrimages made to his grave.

† Although Timūr was a furious Shiāh, his descendants early adopted the Sūnny doctrines. Humāyūn was therefore considered a heterodox Mussulmān, and consequently had no right to enter the mausoleum.

inviting the King to proceed to Cazvin; in consequence of which we marched from Meshehed, and after two journeys reached Nishāpoor; from thence, after six days, we arrived at Subzwār. It so happened that Amyr Shemsaddyn Aly, the governor of Subzwār, was a relation of Myr Berkē, between whom and the King there existed a great intimacy; on which account we remained in that city for forty days; thence, in three days, we reached Damghān, and thence, in two more days, proceeded to Bustām; thence to Semnān, thence to the fort of Ayhzvār, thence to the fountain of Alhāk, thence to the fort of Mesmyeh, where we encamped under a large walnut-tree. While his Majesty was admiring the prospect from this situation, he saw a messenger advancing quickly towards him. When the man came up and made his salutation, the King said, "whence come you?" he replied, "from the fortress of *Bezan Suger*;" the King said, "have you any thing for me?" the man replied, "yes, I have;" the King said, "bring it:" on which he gave into his Majesty's hands a letter from Myrzā Solimān, Chief of Badukhshān. The King having read the letter, said, "these people are very extraordinary *foster brothers*, witness the impropriety of their conduct to my late father (Baber), and are now guilty of want of loyalty towards me, for the foster brother (Kukē) of Myrzā Solimān, named Allah Kūly Inderaby, has seized by order of Kamrān the Myrzā Solimān with all his family, and carried them to Kabul." His Majesty then wrote an answer to the letter, the contents of which were, "Accept my blessing, and be hopeful. Please God, in a short time our affairs will improve." Having sealed the letter, he gave it to the messenger, and added, "give my compliments to Myrzā Solimān, and say I am sensible that he suffers all this inconvenience on my account; but let him be hopeful that every thing will yet turn out according to our wishes."*

After the second prayers we again marched; and as it happened that the King always travelled with a bottle of lemon juice, when we (the servants) were about to mount our horses, the Mehter (Groom) Dulā said, "give me the bottle, and when you are mounted I will return it to you." The humble servant Jouher, *Aftabchy*, would not agree; on which the Groom said, "it

* The Orientals seldom commit their sentiments to writing: the letter was therefore merely complimentary, and the verbal message is the important communication.

does not signify; after I have got on my horse I will take up the bottle." Having mounted, he attempted to do so, when it dropt from his hand and was broken. When we arrived at a certain place it was about the time of evening prayer, and as soon as his Majesty had performed his ablutions, he called for the *lemon juice*, in order to make some Sherbet; it was therefore requisite to explain that the bottle had been broken. The King was very angry, and ordered that the Groom and I should travel in future on foot. After we had marched about two coss, his Majesty kindly said, "the fault was not Jouher's, therefore let him mount; but the Groom shall walk all the way."

We soon after came to the fountain of *Savuk Belāk*, and from thence to the fort of *Ders*. At this place another letter arrived from the sovereign of Persia, stating that he was at Cazvin, and that the King should now send forward Byram Beg as his ambassador. In consequence of this message, Byram Beg was despatched, attended by ten horsemen to the imperial presence. In a few days after his arrival at court, Shāh Tahmāsp ordered him to cut off his hair, and wear a Persian cap; Byram Beg represented that he was the servant of another person, and could only obey his orders. The monarch was very angry, and said, "you may do as you please;" but in order to frighten him into compliance commanded some prisoners to be brought up and executed in his presence. Shāh Tahmāsp then marched to the fountain of *Jeky Jeky*, and wrote to the King Humāyūn to remain where he was till he should send for him; but sent Bubek Beg to be *Mehmander* to his Majesty.

Some time afterwards another order arrived from the Shāh Tahmāsp that the King should advance to Cazvin, and having rested there for three days, might then come and pay his respects to the monarch.

In consequence of this invitation his Majesty left Ders; and when he reached Cazvin,* the governor of that city came out to meet the King, and lodged him with his suite in one of the palaces of the Persian monarch. On the first day a great entertainment was given to his Majesty in the house of the governor; the second day, the Cazy had the pleasure of exhibiting his

* Kazvin or Cazvin, formerly a magnificent city, but now in ruins, in consequence of an earthquake. See Morier's Travels, page 254.

hospitality; and on the third day, the principal inhabitants had the honour of supplying the feast.

The day following his Majesty left Cazvin in the afternoon, and travelled all night; towards morning, the King being tired, ordered his attendants to look out for a place where there was water, that he might halt; whilst we were employed in searching for water, intelligence was brought that Byram Beg (the King's ambassador) was approaching. Shortly after the aforesaid personage arrived, and had the honour of paying his respects; and represented, "that the stage or place of halting was very near at hand;" but the King said, "he would not then proceed any further."

In short the day having now broke, the King, having performed his ablutions, and said his morning prayers, fell asleep. Shortly after the Persian (bildars) pioneers, who were employed in smoothing the road, began to sing in their usual manner: their noise awoke his Majesty; and supposing that they were his own people, he ordered that they should be silenced, as he had been travelling all night, and therefore wished to sleep; the humble servant *Jouher* represented "that they were the pioneers of the Persian monarch, who were repairing the road to the next stage, and could not be interrupted."

The King then ordered me to call Byram Beg; when the aforesaid person came, he represented that the officers deputed by the Persian monarch were now approaching to meet his Majesty, and it was requisite to prepare for their reception: in consequence the King, having bathed and dressed, and the tents being pitched, sat in the Divan Khanē.

In a short time the deputies of the Princes came; after those a deputation of the *Syeds*,* and were particularly noticed: after this the King mounted his horse, and advanced. He was soon after met by the retinues of the Princes and Nobility. But when Sām Myrzā (the son of Shāh Tahmāsp) arrived within the distance of the flight of an arrow from his Majesty, he alighted from his horse; on which the King also alighted, and they embraced each other with the greatest respect and friendship; after which ceremony the Prince returned to where he had alighted, and again mounted his horse. Immediately after this Bahram Myrzā (third brother of Shāh Tahmāsp) came, and having brought with him a dress of honour and a *Gezaleh* (un-

* Descendants of Muhammed.

broke) horse, the master of the ceremonies having arranged the ranks, and spread a carpet, his Majesty was then clothed in the dress, except the cap,* which he would not put on; and, having mounted the unbroke horse, proceeded. It so happened that this wild horse, which the Turcomans (Persians) had brought to try his Majesty's skill in horsemanship, was perfectly tractable, which astonished them all exceedingly, and was considered an auspicious omen. After this the *Kūrjy Bashy*, and a number of inferior people mounted on Carmanian horses, came and made their salute; the object of their being introduced was, to prove that all the Persians, whether of high or low rank, were all on a footing with our King,

When his Majesty entered the paradise-like court of the monarch of Persia, the latter advanced to the edge of the carpet, where the two Kings embraced; after which the Persian monarch placed Humāyūn to his right, and they sat down on the same cushion. He then made several kind enquiries respecting his health, and the circumstances of his journey. He then said, "you must put on the Persian cap;" Humāyūn replied, "that a Taj (crown) is an emblem of greatness; I will with pleasure wear it." Tahmāsp then with his own hands placed the cap on the King's head; on which all the trumpets of the royal band sounded, and all the Nobility, having prostrated themselves, said, "God be praised!" such is their custom.

The King then requested that the Princes might all be seated, but the Persian monarch replied, "that would be contrary to our regulations."

After this, orders were given for the entertainment to be brought in; but the Persian monarch desired that the King's *Suferchy* (butler) might lay the table cloth; on which Yakūb (the butler) came forward and spread the cloth, and the two Kings sat down to eat: when they had finished, the trumpets were again sounded, and the attendants prostrated themselves. But

* Taj, properly Taji Hyder, a tiara of crimson silk, wrought with gold, and richly ornamented with jewels, worn by the kings of Persia, so called from Hyder, the father of Shāh Ismael, by whom it was first adopted. It is of a high conical shape, and divided into twelve segments, in honour of the twelve *Imāms* from whom he claimed descent. In the course of time the Persian officers and soldiers were ordered to wear caps of this pattern, from which they were nicknamed by the Turks, *Kuzel Bash*, red heads. The natives of Hindūstān have a great dislike to caps or hats; but why Humāyūn, who was the son of a Tartar, should have objected, is extraordinary, unless its being the invention of a *Shiāh*.

the particular object of the present ceremony was to return thanks, that the Almighty God had brought so great a Prince as Humāyūn to take refuge at the foot of the imperial throne.

After some other ceremonies, Shāh Tahmāsp said, " your Majesty's abode is to be either with the Prince Bahram or the minister Budder Khān," he then gave him leave to retire. The Prince Bahram then took the King to his house, where, having enjoyed the hot-bath, he had his hair cut off; and the Prince having sent him three honorary dresses, put one of them on; after which they passed the night in feasting and carousing.

The next day the Persian monarch marched to the city of Sultanyeh;* and as he was passing the King's residence in the morning, his Majesty came to the door and made his salutation; but as it was not returned in a polite manner the King was much hurt, and on his arrival at Sultanyeh went and seated himself in the dome of Sultān Mohammed Khodabundeh, the founder of the Shiāhs in Persia, and began to reproach himself for having sought protection with Shāh Tahmāsp, whose behaviour was not sufficiently courteous.

It further happened, that one day when a large quantity of wood had been sent to the King's residence for the use of the followers, Shāh Tahmāsp sent a message to his Majesty, saying, " unless he and all his adherents would become Shiāhs, he would make a funeral pile for them with that wood."† (See Sir J. Malcolm's panegyric in Advertisement.)

The King returned the message, " that he and his adherents were all firmly attached to their own religion, and would not deviate therefrom; that the Persian monarch might do as he pleased, but that their lives were in the hands of God, without whose permission no injury could reach them, and on his protection they alone trusted."

Thus his Majesty continued firm in his faith, and only requested that he and his followers might be permitted to proceed on their pilgrimage to Mecca; to this it was replied, " that he, Shāh Tahmāsp, would shortly draw his armies against the Sūnnies (the Turks) and annihilate them, but that as

* Formerly a fine city, but now in ruins, in consequence of an earthquake. See Morier's Travels, page 257.

† The animosity between the Sūnnies and Shiāhs is as great, as that which formerly existed between the Papists and Protestants. See Preface to Sale's Korān.

Humāyūn had entered Persia of his own accord, he must now adopt the religion of that country, or take the consequences."

Soon after this event Cazy Jehan, the agent of Tahmāsp, who was a highly respectable person, waited on his Majesty, and said, "you are not alone; there are seven hundred *Sūnnies* here, who will all share your fate; but circumstances now require that you should temporise with your oppressors; and if they importune you, from which God and the Prophet protect you! you must say, that being helpless, you will do as they wish." The King said, "what is their object? bring it to me in writing." Some time after, the Cazy came again, and brought three papers from Shāh Tahmāsp; the King having read two of them pushed them away; but when he had read the third he got up, came to the door of the tent, and was about to call out to his people, when the Cazy followed and begged him to be quiet; that there was now no remedy, and that he must temporise; after which the King became more tranquil, and signed one of the papers which the Cazy carried to the Persian monarch.

Some time after this nefarious transaction, Shāh Tahmāsp ordered a hunting party, and directed Cazy Jehan to attend his Majesty. In the course of three days a great number of animals were surrounded, and many of them killed; but it so happened that several deer made their escape at that part of the circle where we were; for each of which the Persian demanded a *fine* of a horse and one *Tuman*.*

The next day Shāh Tahmāsp gave orders that the Prince Bahram should escort the King to see the Throne of Solimān (ruins of Persepolis); in consequence of which we marched all night, and arrived there early in the morning. The Prince then proposed, that as there were a number of animals enclosed there, the King should amuse himself in shooting.† We, therefore, continued our sport till after mid-day, when the King being very tired, alighted to say his prayers; but when he performed his ablutions, the only

* About one pound sterling.

† The mode of hunting practised by the Persian monarchs was by sending an army, principally of cavalry, to surround a district, and drive all the animals of it to a particular spot, where a wooden enclosure had been previously made. It is related in the History of Timūr, that during his invasion of Russia, his army lived for many days on the animals thus collected.

persons of his attendants then present were myself and the butler; his Majesty then ordered me to *champoo* him, which I did till he was recovered from his fatigue; after which he again mounted his horse, and proceeded to join the army.

It was customary with his Majesty always to carry his valuable diamonds and rubies in a purse in his pocket; but when he was performing his ablutions he generally laid them on one side; he had done so this day, and forgot them: it so happened that when the King was gone, and the humble servant *Jouher* was about to remount his horse, he saw a green-flowered purse lying on the ground, and a pen-case by the side of it: he immediately took them up, and as soon as he had overtaken the King, presented them. When his Majesty saw these articles he was amazed and astonished, and said, "Oh, my boy, you have done me the greatest favour possible; if these had been lost, I should have ever been subject to the *meanness* (rezalet) of this Persian monarch: do you in future take care of them."

Now the reason that his Majesty kept these diamonds and rubies about his person was, that he had formerly entrusted his valuables to Rūshen Beg, who had been guilty of dishonesty; on which account the King thought it too great a temptation to be given in charge of any other servant.

Whilst we were on our return to the camp, his Majesty took the opportunity of viewing the ruins of Persepolis. Among other curious things we saw a cave, hollowed out of a mountain, in which they used to confine state prisoners. After viewing this wonderful place, the King proceeded to the camp, and arrived there as they were saying the evening prayers.

The next morning the King again joined the hunters, and, having proceeded to a place about four *coss* from the Tukhti Solimān, began the sport; but the orders of Shāh Tahmāsp were, that no person but himself and the King should discharge an arrow without express permission. After a short time, a deer came bounding towards his Majesty; when the Persian monarch called out, "now, Humāyūn, let us see how you shoot." On which his Majesty discharged his arrow, which struck the animal behind the ear, and it fell struggling on the ground; at which all the Persians were astonished, and said, "certainly Humāyūn will be a fortunate prince." The party soon after returned to the tents, and nine deer were sent as a present to the King.

We remained several days encamped on the hunting grounds; during this time his Majesty ordered his diamonds and rubies to be brought to him; and having selected the largest diamond, placed it in a mother-of-pearl box; he then added several other diamonds and rubies; and having placed them on a tray, gave them in charge of Byram Beg to present them to the Persian monarch, with a message, "that they were brought from Hindūstān purposely for his Majesty."*

When Shāh Tahmāsp saw these precious stones he was astonished, and sent for his jewellers to value them. The jewellers declared they were above all price; on which the Persian signified his acceptance, and conferred on Byram Beg the title of *Khān*, with permission to use the kettle-drum and standard. The diploma and insignia were sent the next day; but from that time, for two months, there was no intercourse of any kind between the monarchs.

CHAPTER XV.

Of other causes of dissention between Shāh Tahmāsp and his Majesty Humāyūn.
A. H. 951.—A. D. 1544.

The subjects which caused the dissention between the two sovereigns were these: first, some of the disaffected nobility of Hindūstān, who, although servants of the King, had taken part with the Prince Kamrān, and who had afterwards gone on the pilgrimage to Mecca, returned from thence by the route of Persia, viz. Rūshen Beg *Kukeh* (foster brother), Khuajē Ghāzy Diwān, and Sultān Muhammed (the spearman), all of whom having obtained access to the Persian monarch, insinuated that Humāyūn had not talents for a king; in consequence of which his brothers had not supported him: they also proposed that, if Shāh Tahmāsp would imprison his *guest*, and

* When Humāyūn took Agra, he found there the family of Rajā Bickermajeet of Gualior, who had been killed in the battle. In consequence of his kind treatment to the prisoners, they presented him with a quantity of jewels; among these was a famous diamond, weighing eight mishkals, which he offered to his father, who returned it to him: its value was incalculable. This probably was the diamond he presented to Tahmāsp. Memoirs of Baber, page 308.

entrust *them* with an army, they would soon take Candahar,* and deliver it over to his Majesty.

The second cause of ill will was this; some of the Turkoman officers said to their monarch, "that Sultān Baber, the father of Humāyūn, had very unjustly put to death one of their countrymen, named Jennum Beg, and that if his Majesty should order any of them to assist Humāyūn in the recovery of his dominions, he would probably murder them in the same treacherous manner." But there was a third, and more powerful cause of offence, of a long standing, which was this: soon after Humāyūn had defeated Behader-Shāh, of Gujerāt (A. D. 1535), and had returned to his capital, Agra, he was one day amusing himself with *divining arrows*.† He wrote his own name on twelve of the first class of arrows, and the name of Shāh Tahmāsp on twelve of the second class; and this anecdote was by some means communicated to the Persian monarch. In consequence, while the two Kings were one day seated together, Shāh Tahmāsp said to Humāyūn, "be so good as explain the reason of your selecting arrows of the *second class* for me on such an occasion;" the King frankly replied, "the fact is, that I then looked to the extent of our mutual dominions; and as Persia at that time was only of half the extent of the kingdom of Hindūstān, I therefore considered you as inferior to myself." Tahmāsp then said, in an ill natured manner, "it was a consequence of your foolish vanity, that you could not properly govern those *extensive* dominions; you were therefore driven away by the *villagers*, and left your wife and family captives:" the King replied, "we are all under the controul of fate, and must willingly submit to the decrees of the Almighty." With this answer the Persian monarch appeared satisfied. [Quotation from the Korān.]

"God is omnipotent over all his works, but the greater part of mankind "do not understand."

Some time after this conversation, the Persian monarch consulted with his brother, Bahram Myrzā, respecting the destruction (helakyt) of the King

* Candahar being a frontier garrison between the two countries had frequently changed masters, and was always coveted by the Persians.

† A mode of predicting future events, in use among the Arabs and other Muhammedans.

Humāyūn. On hearing this proposal, the Myrzā was so much afflicted that he shed tears; he afterwards went to his sister, and said to her, "the King Humāyūn has sought refuge with the Seffy family, and has long partaken with me of the *same salt*, and our brother has now made me such and such proposals."*

When the Princess heard this discourse she also began to weep. Just at this time the Persian monarch entered his sister's apartment; on which Bahram Myrzā made his salutation and retired. The monarch then sat down, and asked the Princess the cause of her crying; she replied, "I am lamenting our adverse fate." He asked, "what more prosperity can you wish for, than that you now enjoy?" she answered, "I am constantly employed in prayers for your welfare: are you not already encompassed by enemies? and are you not engaged in contest with the Turks, the Uzbegs, the Georgians, and the Russians? and I hear you are now about to raise up other enemies by your intentions of injuring Muhammed Humāyūn, whose son and brothers will one day seek revenge. If you will not support him, at least permit him to go away, that he may apply for assistance somewhere else." The Persian monarch was much affected by the address of his sister, and said, "my Chiefs have been giving me unworthy advice; but what you have suggested is certainly more dignified and praise worthy."

Shortly after this, Shāh Tahmāsp sent the King an invitation to visit him at his hunting encampment; he went, and arrived about mid-day, and remained till late in the evening; during which time the Persian monarch behaved with the greatest kindness; and as our King was about to take leave, said, "Keep your mind at ease, for I shall very soon send you to your own country in a proper manner. Oazy Jehan will mention certain subjects, to which I request you will pay attention;" on which the King offered up prayers for the prosperity of his Majesty.

The two monarchs then mounted to return to their tents; but after riding

* About the time that Major Yule procured this MS. there was a descendant of the Seffy family residing at Lucknow, who received a small pension from the Nuwab Assuf addowleh, and bore the title of *Persian Prince*. Major Yule having lent him the MS. he wrote on the margin at this passage, "The author has here been guilty of falsehood, or he must have been deranged, as this circumstance has never been mentioned by any other historian."

some distance our King was obliged to alight, having no other attendants with him than his groom. When he had been some time absent, and as it was very dark, Shāh Tahmāsp was alarmed, and said, " what is become of Humāyūn ? I fear some of my Turkomans* may hurt him ;" and immediately ordered one of the two torch-bearers that were before him to go in search of the King. The Kūrchy, carrying the lighted torch, wandered about, and kept calling in the Tūrky language. At length the King heard his voice, and sent the groom to say he was coming. Several of the Persian attendants then came, and said their master was enquiring most particularly for him: the King then joined the Persian monarch, and they rode together till they came to some tents, when Shāh Tahmāsp asked whose tents they were; and on being informed they were the King's, he then shook his Majesty by the hand, wished him a good night, and went to his own pavilion.

About midnight the King complained of being very hungry; on which some of the Persian servants who were in attendance went and informed Shāh Tahmāsp of the circumstance, who immediately ordered that a supper should be sent to him. Nine dishes were very shortly brought, and his Majesty regaled himself most heartily, and afterwards went to bed.

The next day the Persian monarch went to visit a valley, or pass in that neighbourhood, but we halted; his Majesty therefore took that opportunity of assembling his *Hindūstāny* servants, and informed us of the very great kindness of Shāh Tahmāsp, and of the various conversations he had had with him; he added, " Cazy Jehan will speak to you also on a certain subject (conversion)." On hearing this discourse all the servants raised their hands in prayer for his Majesty, and were all highly delighted at his prospects. He then ordered us to attend him when he went to join the Persian monarch.

The next morning his Majesty again joined the hunters, who had formed an enclosure of wild animals in the vicinity of the ruins of Persepolis; and so numerous were the deer that they had not room to escape; so that frequently the two Kings having seized the horns of a stag, pulled him out of the enclosure and let him go; in short, the whole day passed in hunting

* As a great part of the Persian armies was composed of soldiers from the *Türky* hordes, they are frequently, but improperly, called Turkomans. See Morier's Travels, pages 240 and 288.

and shooting, and in the evening the party returned to the tents, which were then pitched among the aforesaid ruins.

All this time Shāh Tahmāsp was considering of the best mode of giving a sumptuous entertainment to the King; in consequence of which he had given orders to his officers to make a selection of every thing that might be requisite for the purpose.

On the fifth day after his Majesty's arrival at Persepolis, he was informed that Shāh Tahmāsp had passed judgement on the conduct of Rūshen Beg, Khuajē Ghāzy, and Sultān Muhammed, who had endeavoured to sow dissention between the monarchs, as was formerly related (see page 68), and had ordered these persons to be confined. [Extract from the Korān.]

" He who digs a pit for his neighbour shall fall into it himself."

In short, Shāh Tahmāsp commanded that some of the longest ropes should be taken from the tents, and that these three culprits should be let down into the caverns or pits, called the prison of the Diwān of Solimān, before described; but if the ropes were not long enough to reach the bottom, they (the culprits) might be hauled up again.

When this circumstance was communicated to the prisoners, Rūshen Beg wrote a petition to the King, acknowledging his crime, expressing his contrition, and imploring him in the name of his mother, whose milk he had sucked,* to pardon and intercede for him. In consequence of which, the good-natured King wrote, and implored the Persian monarch, by the tomb of his father Ismael, to release the prisoners. When Shāh Tahmāsp read the letter he was astonished, and said, " doubtless Muhammed Humāyūn is a man of the greatest forbearance and clemency, thus to intercede for wretches who have endeavoured to do him the greatest injury." He therefore gave orders that the prisoners should be delivered over to his Majesty, that he might do with them as he pleased.

About a week after this affair, Shāh Tahmāsp sent an invitation to the King to come to the entertainment prepared for him. Three hundred tents had been fetched for this occasion, and twelve bands of military music stationed in different places, all of which struck up when his Majesty advanced; and the whole of the ground was covered with the imperial carpets.

* He was the King's foster brother.

On the first day there was a great profusion of every kind of eatables, and dresses of honour were conferred on the King, and on all the guests.

On the second day Shāh Tahmāsp, having seated the King close to him, told him that the tents, and every thing he saw, were at his service, and desired him to mention any thing else that he wished for; he also told him, that he had ordered his son to attend him, with 12,000 chosen cavalry, to restore him to his dominions; he further said, upon your arrival at Systān, you shall yourself muster these troops, and be convinced of their efficiency.

The Persian monarch then rose, and placing his right hand on his breast, added, "O, Humāyūn, if I have been deficient in ought, I trust to your generosity to excuse it."

On the third day the monarchs amused themselves in shooting with bows and arrows; but when night came on, a great company was assembled, and various kinds of wine and liquors were introduced; before each of the guests was placed a bottle and a goblet, that he might help himself; so that there was no occasion for servants to attend (in order that they need not be under any restraint).

As it had been determined that the camp was to break up next day, his Majesty rose early in the morning, but before his departure went to pay his respects to the Persian monarch, and found him seated in the open air on a small carpet, doubled up; and when his Majesty alighted from his horse, as there was no place for him to sit down, a Moghul, Muhammed Kushky, having cut off the cover of his quiver, spread it for his Majesty to sit on.

The King, pleased with this attention, said to him, "who are you?" to which he replied, "I am a Moghul;" the King said, "you may continue in my service;" the man replied, "I am unworthy of it; but my master is already in your Majesty's service; whenever you shall promote him, I will then become your devoted servant."

After taking leave of Shāh Tahmāsp, the King proceeded towards Tabriz, and halted at a station four coss from Persepolis; but as the Persian monarch had intimated that he expected a feast from him in the Hindūstāny manner of cookery, preparations were in consequence now made for this ceremony, a number of public singers were collected, and various kinds of liquors procured. The Persian monarch, and the guests having been seated, and the cup having repeatedly passed round, a tray of the fruit called the *Royal Sachek* (species unknown), was produced; on which Shāh Tahmāsp said, "who is to divide the *Sacheks?*" the King replied, "whoever your Majesty shall order:" Tahmāsp directed the chief eunuch to do so. The Khuajeh then placed a whole one before the Persian monarch, a whole one before the King, and half a one before each of the other guests,* (or a plate *full* before each of the monarchs.) After this ceremony various kinds of food and drink were presented, and every body heartily participated; but Shāh Tahmāsp was more pleased with the dish of rice and peas (*Dal Khuskē*) than any of the others, it being a mode of cookery unknown in Persia. After dinner both monarchs made a short march.

The next morning the Persian monarch ordered that the King's tents should remain at that station, but that his Majesty might accompany *him* to the next stage. In consequence of which the King rode ten *coss* with Shāh Tahmāsp, and remained with him that night in his pavilion, during which time it rained very hard.

CHAPTER XVI.

Account of the taking leave of the two monarchs, and the departure of the King for Candahar. A. H. 951-2.—A. D. 1544-5.

The next morning, as soon as the rain had ceased, Shāh Tahmāsp stood up, and said, "Now, Humāyūn, you may go, and the blessing of God be with you!" he then presented him with two *apples and a knife*, and placing a ring on the King's finger, gave him his dismissal. He then commanded that the Prince Bahram should accompany his Majesty to the stage where his tents were pitched.

The King having made his obeisance, mounted his horse, and, being accompanied by the Prince and a number of people, proceeded on his journey. When they came within sight of the tents, the Prince requested his dis-

* When Nadir Shāh invaded Dehly, and was seated with Muhammed Shāh, coffee was introduced, and the servant doubtful how to act, presented the cups to the Vizier, who presenting a cup to Muhammed Shāh (his master), requested *him* to present it to the conqueror, by which he avoided giving offence to either party.

missal; upon which the King, having cut an apple in two, gave one piece to Bahram, and eat the other himself: he then drew from his pocket a diamond ring, and gave it to the Prince, saying, "this ring was a keepsake of my mother's, preserve it in remembrance of me; such is my friendship for you, that I would willingly remain with you all my life; but my reputation is at stake, and obliges me to leave you." The Prince replied, "be assured that I will keep the ring in remembrance of your friendship; depart in confidence of success in all your undertakings."

That day the King made a short march, and in three more days reached Tabriz.* We remained there five days, during which time his Majesty visited the bazar of Cæsarea and the dome of Syria, so called from the materials of which it is built, having been brought from Syria. In going through the market he saw two Turks, who having saluted him, he said, in Turkish, "give my compliments to your sovereign;" they replied, in the same language, "most certainly we will." The King then proceeded towards Ardebyl,† and in four nights reached that city, and remained there a whole week. The objects of coming to Ardebyl were, first, to visit the tombs of Shaikh Seffy,‡ upon whom be the peace of God! and of Shāh Ismael; at the gate of which there is a chain, by getting inside of which any culprit is saved from the pursuit of the officers of justice, whatever may have been his crime: the other object was to perform the ceremony of *betrothing* a niece of the Persian monarch, the daughter of Masūm Beg, who had been promised to him.§

After this ceremony his Majesty proceeded to *Derya Kulzum* (the Caspian sea), over which there is constantly a thick fog or mist. Having satisfied his curiosity, he returned to Ardebyl; from thence he came to Kherdebyl, from thence to Tarūn, thence to Serkhāb, and from thence, after several marches, reached Cazvin.

It so happened that the Persian monarch, who had been making an ex-

* The capital of the province of Azerbijān, and now the residence of Abbas Myrzā, N. Lat. 38,10. E. Long. 46,37.

† See Edinburgh Gazetteer.

‡ The founder of the family. See Advertisement, page 57. His tomb was an asylum for culprits.

§ As we do not hear any more of this marriage, it was probably never consummated.

cursion in the country, returned the same day to Cazvin, and seeing the King's tents, asked to whom they belonged; when told they were the encampment of King Humāyūn, he said, "what! has he not yet left this country?" He then ordered Mehter Khyaly to come and desire that his Majesty would make a march of twelve ferseng (leagues.) In consequence of this message the King made several marches, and had nearly reached the fort of Aris, when four horsemen were seen on the Desert, who came up and killed Yakūb the *Suferchy* (butler.) As soon as the King was informed of the circumstance, he ordered the men to be pursued; but when our people came up with them, they said, "why are you following us? we have but acted by Shāh Tahmāsp's orders."

Now the reason of the murder of Yakūb was this: there had been a quarrel between him and the chamberlain, Hussyn Aly Aka, in consequence of the Persian monarch having one day sent to the King a present of several swords, one of which Hussyn Aly took for himself; Yakūb having obtained information of this dishonesty, mentioned it to his Majesty, in revenge for which the Aka complained to his master, Shāh Tahmāsp, that Yakūb had spoken disrespectfully of the *Persian cap.** This was the real cause of the murder of poor Yakūb, which much annoyed his Majesty.

After this the King continued his march to Sebzvar, and at this place ordered that the Begum, with all the heavy baggage, should proceed by the route of Tebesh, (or *Tubbus of the map,*) while he should go to Meshehed, and again visit the tomb of the Imām Aly, son of Musa, "upon whom be the grace of God!" His Majesty accordingly marched to Meshehed, and received back the *bow,* together with the string, which he had suspended on the tomb; by which circumstance he was much gratified, it being a proof that the Imām or his servants were auspicious to his affairs.

During the period of seven days that his Majesty remained at the holy sanctuary, it snowed the greater part of the time.

At length the snow having ceased, the King marched to Ravut Terk, and from thence to Lengur, where is situated the tomb of Shāh-Casim-Anvar; from thence to the fort of Kāh or Gāh, where one of the twelve holy *Imāms* disappeared. It is said that even to this day, the sounds of drums and

* See page 64.

trumpets are heard from the tomb; and every person who has any wish ungratified, has only to repair thither, and having offered up his petition in a pious and humble manner, the Lord God causes it to be fulfilled. After remaining there one night, his Majesty proceeded to Tebesh (or Tubbus), and from thence after several marches entered Systān.

CHAPTER XVII.

The King re-enters his own dominions, and takes the fortresses of Bost and Candahar, &c.
A. H. 951-2.—A. D. 1544-5.

Having entered the province of Systān, his Majesty halted for fifteen days; the reason of which was, that when he took leave of the Persian monarch, the latter had told him that on his arrival in Systān, the army sent to restore him to his dominions would assemble there for his inspection. In consequence of these orders, the chiefs having assembled from different quarters, the King took a muster of the troops, and found that instead of 12,000 there were actually 14,000 cavalry present at the review.

After the business of the muster had been settled, the King said to the Persian chiefs, "at the distance of about thirty miles from hence is the fortress of Bost,* commonly called *Medain*, and formerly the residence of Nushirvan the Just, which is now commanded by Myr Khelj, one of the officers of Myrzā Askery: I wish you to proceed thither, and summon him to give up the fort; if he does not, you must take it by force, and even put him and the garrison to death." The chiefs replied, "this is contrary to the orders we received from our monarch;" the King said, "I will write to Shāh Tahmāsp on the subject."

But on the arrival of the King in the vicinity of Bost, Myr Khelj having suspended a scimitar on his neck, came out, paid his respects, and was graciously received; from thence his Majesty marched towards Candahar; and on his arrival there sent Byram Beg as his ambassador to the Prince Kamrān at Kabul. But as Myrzā Askery, who commanded the fortress of Candahar, would not give it up, the consequence of which was a severe contest, and

* It is situated on the river Hyrmund, about 32,20 N. Lat.

several officers were killed; so that the King finding he could not take the fort by assault, gave orders to lay regular siege to it, and to erect batteries against it.

During this time Alek or Aleg Myrzā, a cousin of the King's, who had been confined by the Prince Kamrān, and had been given in charge to Shere Afgun, persuaded his keeper to escape with him, and they both arrived in safety at the royal camp.

One day while the King was examining the progress of the siege, having climbed a hill, he saw a part of the building in the fort where the council chamber of the Prince was situated, and gave orders that a great gun should be pointed against it; when the gun was discharged, the shot struck the lattice work of the council chamber, which caused a great uproar in the place, and frightened the garrison exceedingly.

About this time the Prince Kamrān wrote a letter from Kabul to Khuandzadeh, sister of the late Emperor Baber, requesting her to intercede with the King for Myrzā Askery; in consequence of which the aforesaid lady wrote to his Majesty begging he would pardon Askery; which being granted, the Myrzā came out of the fort, and had the honour of paying his respects (*kuddum busy*).

In short as soon as Candahar was taken, the Persian chiefs claimed the treasure for their master, Shāh Tahmāsp;* or, if this was refused, they demanded the Prince Askery should be sent to him. The King would not acknowledge the justness of the *claim*, but said the money should be sent as an offering of friendship. He therefore went into the fort accompanied by some of the Persians and all his own attendants; amongst whom was the humble servant *Jouher Aftabchy;* and, shortly after alighting at Myrzā Askery's house, gave orders that the treasury should be opened, and the money brought out and examined: he then, in presence of the son of the Persian monarch, of Shāh Kuly Khān, governor of Kerman, of the general Bedagh Khān, of Hussyn Sultān, governor of Senjāb, and of Ahmed Sultān, governor of Systān, directed that the chests should be locked and sealed with his own and the seals of the above-mentioned chiefs; and

* It was one of the stipulations between the two monarchs that in future Candahar should belong to Persia.

having made over the treasure to them, came out of the fort (leaving them in possession.)

The Persian chiefs then deliberated, not only upon sending off the treasure to Persia, but also of seizing Myrzā Askery, and sending him as a hostage to Shāh Tahmāsp for their own safe return.

On hearing this report the King ordered a muster of all his own troops; and many of the Hindūstānies having by this time joined him, they all passed in review. This event alarmed the Persians, and they said among themselves, "the intentions of the King towards us are not good; as his father Baber delivered over Nejem Beg into the hands of the Uzbegs, who put him to death, he probably means to do us some mischief." They therefore sent off the treasure to the distance of twelve coss, and by continued marches delivered it in safety to Shāh Tahmāsp, who was so much gratified by the circumstance, that he sent an honorary dress and a rich dagger to his Majesty, which were duly received and honoured.

After the fort had been made over to the Persians, the King left the vicinity of Candahar, and encamped for a month at Khuljeh Bāgh; but the Persian officers being jealous of the King's remaining so long in their neighbourhood, took measures to prevent our camp being supplied with provisions.

On hearing of this circumstance, his Majesty called a council of his officers to deliberate on what measures were best to be taken. The council were of opinion, that the first object was to procure a supply of horses to mount our men; and as it was known that the Persian garrison of Candahar had sold their horses to some merchants who were encamped with them outside the walls of the fort, it would be advisable to seize them. In consequence of this advice the King, preceded by several officers, returned by a forced march to Candahar, seized seventeen hundred horses, and immediately returned to his camp, which he reached at midnight.

The next morning he had all the horses brought out, and marked with the royal stamp; after which he called for the merchants, and gave them his bond to repay the price the first opportunity. He then selected one hundred and fifty horses for the Princes Hindal and Yadgār Myrzā, and divided the remainder among the troops, according to their respective ranks.

CHAPTER XVIII.

Account of the death of the Persian Prince, of the recapture of Candahar, and of the King's journey to Kabul. A. H. 952.—A. D. 1545.

After the division of the horses, the King was making preparation to march towards Kabul, when private information was brought to him that the young Persian Prince* had died in Candahar. He immediately called a council of his chiefs, when it was resolved to endeavour to recover that fortress. The King asked how it could possibly be done? Hajy Muhammed Khān Kūky replied, "leave the business to me, and I will engage to do it." The King having agreed, gave him his blessing. The Hajy then marched with a select body of troops at midnight; and having arrived at Candahar, just as they were opening the gates of the town in the morning, took the Persians by surprise and entered the place; but the general, Bedāgh Khān, took refuge in the citadel.

When the King arrived within a few miles of Candahar he was met by a servant of Hajy Muhammed, who informed him of his master's success, and congratulated his Majesty on the capture of the town. On entering the city the King took up his residence in the Akshai bastion, and sent a message to the Persian general, asking him why he had endeavoured to conceal the death of the young Prince; that his father had given the boy to him; that he considered the boy as his own son, and had he been informed, should immediately have come to perform the funeral ceremonies: he added, "I will not allow you to go out of the gate, nor will I permit you to visit me, as I fear my Moghuls may injure you; but you may go away unmolested on my part." In consequence of this hint, Bedāgh Khān, during the night, had part of the wall at the back of the fort thrown down, and marched quietly off.

The King then divided the district of Candahar among his principal officers; but as the Persians had collected the revenues for the Rubby or spring quarter, he permitted them to take only the remaining three quarters, with which they were satisfied.

* The Author does not give the name; but in Dow's History of Hindūstān he is called Murād.

After this he sent the Begum with all her attendants into the fort, which he left under charge of Byram Khān, and then proceeded towards Kabul.

During the course of the journey to Kabul, his Majesty received letters from several of the chiefs of Kamrān Myrzā, expressing their loyalty, and encouraging him to proceed. When we reached the town of Tyry, which is situated in the Hezareh mountains, and was the Jagyr of Aleg Myrzā, the Prince Hindal and Terdy Beg came and paid their respects to his Majesty.

At this place information was brought that the Prince Kamrān had marched from Kabul, and had taken possession of the passes: on hearing this, the King ordered the troops to put on their armour, and proceeded towards Kabul. It was shortly after reported that Casim Berlas, the Prince's general, had advanced as far as the pass of the Ass (Hemar) with the intention of giving battle; on which his Majesty ordered Hajy Muhammed to advance with a considerable force and disperse the rebels. The royal troops having reached the aforesaid pass, attacked the rebels with such vigour, that they in a short time took to flight, and, by the blessing of God, his Majesty obtained a complete victory. The King then advanced to the pass, and was congratulated by all the officers on his success.

About this time several of the chiefs interceded with his Majesty to pardon the Prince Kamrān: the King replied, "let us go on, and see how matters are likely to end; I will then decide:" he then ordered the drum of march to be beaten, and proceeded on his journey. During this time Allah Kuly waited on his Majesty, and, in tears, represented that his father, Hyder Sultān, had been called to the Divine mercy. On hearing this the King embraced him, and said, "Please God, I will in future be your father, and will take care of you; be not afflicted, but act as a man." With this consolation the young man returned home. The King then continued his march to Khoujeh Bastan, which was three coss beyond the place where the battle had occurred.

At this place he was met by two holy men, who said they were come to make peace between the King and his brother. On hearing this his Majesty alighted, and embraced them in the most affectionate manner; he afterwards joined them in the morning prayers, and then civilly dismissed them. On departing, they said, "we are most anxious to effect a peace; if the Prince

Kamrān will attend to our advice, we will return by mid-day; but if we do not return, your Majesty will act as you think proper." The holy men could not prevail on the Prince to submit, and therefore returned to Kabul; so that when the prescribed time had elapsed without their appearance, his Majesty ordered Rosheng, the keeper of the wardrobe, to go with the following message to his brother, "*We* are travellers, you are resident; if you will wait on us, it will be according to rule; but if not, *we* will come to you." Rosheng was graciously received by the Prince, and delivered the message word for word; but as the Myrzā was then performing his ablutions, he merely said, "that he was coming."

Rosheng however discovered that the followers of Kamrān were in a very perturbed state, and that many of them were making their escape to Kabul; he, therefore, came away without waiting to take leave, and reported all he had seen to his Majesty. On hearing these circumstances, the King ordered a body of seven hundred lancers, under the command of the Prince Hindal, to advance; and seizing a spear in his own hand, rode on in the midst of them. After a short time he was met by a deputation of Kamrān's chiefs, who came to beg forgiveness, and offer their services.

CHAPTER XIX.

Account of the flight of Kamrān Myrzā towards Bhiker, the taking of Kabul, and of the war between his Majesty and Solimān Myrzā. A. H. 952.—A. D. 1545.

Whilst his Majesty thus advanced in formidable array towards Kabul, the Prince Kamrān being terrified, first retreated to that fortress, and having collected all his family, then proceeded towards Hindūstān.

As soon as the Prince had effected his escape, Carajā Khān, the governor, waited on the King, and requested him to enter the fort, which, although it was then night, he did, and alighted at the *Diwan*, or council room. As his Majesty had not eaten any thing the whole day, he was very hungry, and sent a message by Vasil, the chamberlain, and myself, to Raykē Begum, widow of the late emperor, to request if she had any provisions prepared to send him some.

We went and delivered the message with the King's compliments; the Begum made her acknowledgements, and immediately gave us some beef broth, and a *curry* made of the sáme meat with vegetables. Having carried them to the council room, the chamberlain spread the table-cloth, and laid the supper before his Majesty; but no sooner had he put his spoon into the dishes and found that it was *beef*, than he drew back his hand, and said aloud, "Oh unfortunate Kamrān! was this the mode of your own existence? and did you feed the Asylum of Chastity on the flesh of cows? what! could you not afford to keep a few goats for her subsistence? this is not fit food even for the devout persons who wait on the tomb of our father.* What! could not we, his *four* sons, support his relict as he did?" His Majesty then swallowed a cup full of *Sherbet*, and did not break his fast till next day.

In short, all the officers and chiefs of the Prince Kamrān waited on his Majesty, and were all received in the most gracious manner; after which he ordered the town crier to be sent round the city to proclaim pardon and safety to all the inhabitants. He then made a division of the district in Jagyrs to all his chiefs according to their respective ranks.

As soon as the King found himself peaceably established in Kabul, he sent a *Firmān* to Myrzā Solimān of Badukhshān,† the contents of which were, "I am informed, that in consequence of your friendship for me, my brother, Kamrān, has caused you a great deal of trouble. Now, thank God, the posture of affairs is changed; and as I wish to prove my affection, I request you will favour me with a visit, as I have a longing desire to see you." The Myrzā however would not accept this kind invitation, but wrote back, "that Kamrān had exacted from him a solemn vow, that he would not visit his Majesty till he first had a battle with him."

As the King was then employed in preparation for the circumcision of his son, Muhammed Akber, he at that time took no notice of this insult, but ordered Carajā Beg and some other chiefs to proceed to Candahar, and convoy from thence the Queen, Hemyd Banu Begum, that she might be present on this joyful occasion. During this time his Majesty employed

* Baber was buried at Kabul, which had been his favourite residence.

† He was either a descendant of Jengyz Khān or of Timūr.

himself in sporting on the river Baran,* and on his return encamped in a large garden called *Suret Khanē*, where grand preparations had been made for this indispensable ceremony. The Queen having arrived, the royal throne was raised, and a number of stools were placed near it for the Princes and Nobility. The King then mounted the throne, and all the grandees were seated according to their respective ranks. The Prince Akber was then brought in, and circumcised according to the Mussulmān law; after which dresses of honour were conferred on all the chiefs, and a sumptuous entertainment was given to them and all their attendants.

The King soon after found himself at leisure to think of Myrzā Solimān's affair: in consequence of which he appointed Myr Muhammed Aly to be governor of Kabul, and marched out to the fort of Zuffer, where he mustered his forces, and thence proceeded to Anderāb. The Myrzā Solimān having at the same time advanced, the contending armies met at the village of *Tyrgerān*, and a battle took place; but, through the Divine favour, we gained the victory, and the Myrzā was compelled to flee.

After this event his Majesty marched to *Keshem*, where he remained for three months. Immediately on quitting *Keshem* he was taken ill, and was for one day in so dangerous a state that he was insensible, and several of the chiefs prepared to desert. During this time Carajā Khān fearing a rebellion, confined the Prince Askery in his house. But the Queen, although greatly distressed, personally attended the King, and having squeezed some pomegranates, poured the juice into his mouth, which, through the grace of God, restored him to his senses: he then opened his eyes, and asked the Queen what was the state of affairs; she told him, that every body was in the greatest anxiety and perturbation. He therefore sent for Carajā Khān, and said to him, "I feel much better; go and comfort my people." On this the Khān came out, and informed the chiefs that his Majesty was again quite sensible. In a few days the King recovered, and returned to the fort of Zuffer, whence he despatched Mehter Vasil, and some other officers, to bring from Kabul the tents and arms requisite for marching into Hindūstān.

* The river Baran is described by Baber, in his Memoirs, as abounding with fish and all kinds of wild fowl, page 153.

CHAPTER XX.

An Account of the return of the Prince Kamrān from Bhiker, and of his retaking Kabul by surprise. A. H. 953.—A. D. 1546.

Whilst the King was encamped at Zuffer, the Prince Kamrān having made forced marches from Bhiker, first took the fort of *Tyry*, and put out the eyes of the governor; he then took Ghizni, and slew its governor; afterwards he proceeded rapidly to Kabul, and having found the governor and other officers off their guard, took the place by surprise, and either blinded or put them to death; after which he again got possession of the Prince Muhammed Akber.

On hearing of these lamentable events, the King made peace with Myrzā Solimān, and gave him the fort of Zuffer; but Kundez, which was formerly included in the district of Zuffer, he separated from it, and gave it to the Prince Hindal: he then encouraged his army, and proceeded towards Kabul; but several of the chiefs deserted, and joined Kamrān.

When his Majesty had reached Talicān it snowed heavily for several days, which compelled him to halt at that place for some time; but when the weather cleared up he again marched, and having arrived at Kundez, was hospitably entertained by the Prince Hindal.

At this time Carajā Khān represented to his Majesty, that, in consequence of the desertion of the chiefs, many of the soldiers were wavering in their minds, and that it was requisite to encourage them. His Majesty therefore went amongst the men, spoke kindly to them, and held out hopes to them of better days; and even I, the *humble servant*, successfully used my influence with some of the soldiers.

In short, the King having taken the route of the *Chehar der* (four gates), proceeded towards Kabul: it was then the depth of winter, and such a quantity of snow had fallen that the roads were quite blocked up; we were therefore obliged to ram the snow well down; after which the horses and camels were enabled to move on. When we reached the station of *Charēhkaran*, news arrived that the Prince Kamrān was resolved to risk the consequences of another engagement; we therefore marched on to *Ama Khuatun*. Here the men were ordered to put on their armour, and we advanced in battle array till we came to *Auret Chalak*. Here his Majesty alighted, and having finished his ablutions and prayers, performed some of the ceremonies used in discovering omens, which he found to be auspicious; he, therefore, again mounted his horse, and advanced. When we reached the villages of the Afghāns, Shyr Afgun made his appearance at the head of the advance guard of the rebels, and was immediately attacked by a detachment under the command of the Prince Hindal. Whilst the two parties were warmly engaged, his Majesty, perceiving that the young Prince was nearly left alone, was about to proceed in person to his assistance; but Carajā Khān requested that his Majesty would keep in the rear, and allow *him* to attack the enemy; the King consented; and Carajā having charged the rebels, engaged in single combat with Shyr Afgun: three cuts had been given on either side, when the rebel chief making a violent lunge at his assailant, fell from his horse; Carajā then rode over him, took him prisoner, and brought him to his Majesty, who gave orders that he should be taken care of; but Carajā represented that the prisoner was a deserter and a rebel, and, therefore, ought to be put to death: in consequence of this remonstrance he was beheaded, and the rest of his party fled. The King then lauded Prince Hindal, and thanked the soldiers.

Shortly after this event information was brought that the Prince Kamrān was again endeavouring to escape from Kabul; his Majesty, therefore, gave orders that small parties should be placed on every side of the fort to prevent his egress; spies were also sent into the town to obtain intelligence. The King then went and alighted at the tent of Carajā Khān, when mutual tokens of friendship were exchanged.

At this time the Prince Kamrān sent a message to Carajā, "that he wished to speak to him; and that if he did not come, he should put his son, Sirdar Beg, to death." Carajā represented the circumstance to the King, who said, "if he does, I will be your son;" to which the other replied, "I consider each hair of your Majesty's head worth the life of a son."

The next morning, as soon as the sun rose, the King placed his troops all round the fort, and took post himself at the Eagle's Mount (Kūh Akabyn), whence he had a good view of the fortress, after which he ordered the great guns to be opened against it; but Kamrān having threatened to expose the young Prince Akber to the fire of the cannon, his Majesty forbade their being used, but directed the troops to preserve a strict blockade.

Note.—The long contest between the King and Prince Kamrān is very tiresome; but as it led to a horrid catastrophe it cannot be properly abridged.

CHAPTER XXI.

Account of the escape of the Prince Kamrān from Kabul, and of his Majesty again taking possession of it, with other occurrences of the time. A. H. 954.—A. D. 1547.

After the fortress of Kabul had been besieged in this manner for three months, the Prince Kamrān, taking the advantage of a dark night, effected his escape, and took the route of Zuffer. The King then gained possession of Kabul, but sent the Prince Hindal in pursuit of his brother: he shortly came up with the refugee, and was astonished to find him mounted on the *back of a man* :* he was about to seize Kamrān, who cried out, "if you make me your prisoner the King will certainly take my life, and what will you gain by that?" The Prince was much affected at seeing his brother in that deplorable situation, presented him with a horse, and turned back.

The King, having been much incensed against the inhabitants of Kabul for allowing themselves to be surprised by the rebels, permitted his troops to plunder them for a whole night; after which a crier was sent round the town to order them to desist, and that any person found plundering after that hour should be punished.

The Prince Kamrān having arrived at Zuffer, attempted to take it, but was repulsed by Solimān; he therefore went and took refuge with the Uzbegs, who having assisted him with troops, he returned and laid siege to Kundez, now garrisoned by the Prince Hindal; but having written a note to Hindal, which fell into the hands of the Uzbegs, they suspected a collu-

* It is related by Foster, or some other writer, that through the province of Cashmire this is not an uncommon mode of travelling. The porters are very strong, and have small chairs fitted to their knots or pads: it is said that a porter of Bussora will carry a *pipe* of wine on his back.

sion between the brothers, and effected their retreat; thus Kamrān succeeded in getting possession of Talicān and Zuffer.

About this time an unfortunate difference took place between his Majesty and Carajā Khān, the circumstances of which were nearly these: one day Carajā having urged the King to confer ten *Tumans* (the trifling sum of ten pounds) on a certain officer, his Majesty consented; in consequence of which Carajā wrote the *Perwaneh* (order) on the treasury; but when it was presented, the *Diwan*, Kuajeh Ghazy, refused payment, and represented to the King, " that as he was answerable for the expences of the army, he, therefore, could not allow any other person to interfere." The officer having carried back the *Perwaneh* to Carajā, the latter remonstrated with the King, who not taking any notice of the affair, a coolness ensued between them, and Carajā endeavoured to seduce several other chiefs to desert with him to the Prince Kamrān.* His Majesty having received a hint of these circumstances, and being very desirous of a reconciliation, ordered his son Akber to go to Carajā and the other chiefs to make friends of them, and bring them back with him; but the eunuch, Amber, represented that such a mission for the Prince would be derogatory to the royal dignity, and, perhaps, that they might seize the boy as a *hostage*. The King, therefore, sent a message by another person to Carajā, requesting him to overlook what had passed, and to feel assured that he had the greatest regard for him. Carajā replied, " if such is the case, let him deliver over the *Diwan* to me, that I may take satisfaction." The King sent back another message to him, saying, " you are my vizier and deputy; the *Diwan* is under your controul, and on some other opportunity you can call him to account." Carajā would not be reconciled; but, having persuaded two other chiefs and a party of Moghuls to accompany him, marched off in full armour.

When intelligence of this unlucky affair was brought to the King, he ordered out a party of cavalry, and pursued the deserters in person: he came up with them at a place called *Ashter Keram*, when a skirmish took place; but Carajā soon fled, and joined the Prince Kamrān; on which his Majesty returned to Kabul.

* Humāyūn seems to have been similarly placed with regard to his chiefs as Mary Queen of Scots was.

He then sent a message to Meha Sultān Myrzā (probably a cousin of the late Emperor) to ask his advice. The Myrzā replied, "Kamrān is now puffed up with pride by the junction of Carajā and the other chiefs; but whichever of you first pass the mountain of Hindū Kūsh will be successful." The King immediately said, "Pride must have a fall; if it please God, I will first cross the mountain, and be victorious." He then offered up prayers for his success, and on Tuesday having mounted, he proceeded to the station of *Auret Jalak*, and despatched a messenger to Ghizneh to summon Hajy Muhammed Keshky to join him; who, contrary to the wishes of the other disaffected chiefs, waited on his Majesty.

CHAPTER XXII.

The King seeks for an auspicious omen, and in consequence lays siege to the fort of Talicān, &c. A. H. 955.—A. D. 1548.

It was the custom of his Majesty always to keep a *Cock* in the *Ewry*, for the purpose of awaking the servants early in the morning: it was a beautiful white bird, and the King used frequently to feed it with *raisins:* one day, while his Majesty was standing in the Ewry, he said to himself, "if it is the will of fortune to favour me, the cock will mount upon my shoulder, and evince his delight;" in an instant the bird flew on the King's shoulder, and began to crow; on which his Majesty was much pleased, took the cock in his hands, and put a silver ring on its neck.

The next day we marched to Cara Bāg, thence to Keram, thence to Gūl Behar, thence to Penj sheher,* which is situated in a delightful valley, abounding with all kinds of luxuries, the inhabitants of which are nearly connected with the unbelievers, who wear black clothes (Syāhposhan); but it is considered as a dependency upon Kabul. From this place we again marched, and entered the mountains called Hindū Kūsh (the Hindū slayer); the next day we got through the pass, and encamped on the banks of the river Bengy.

At this place a messenger arrived from the Prince Hindal, bringing a letter

* See Rennell's Map of the places between Delhi and Candahar.

and a present of some fine melons. The next day we marched after morning prayer, and continued our journey till after sun-set, when intelligence was brought that the Prince Hindal was arrived. The Prince was about to dismount to pay his respects, but the King requested he would not take the trouble; in short, they embraced on horseback, and the King spoke to him in the most affectionate manner. During their discourse his Majesty enquired what was become of their brother Kamrān, and the other insurgents? the Prince replied, "that they were in possession of the fort of Zuffer." After travelling a great part of the night, we halted on the bank of the river Helcana.

During the next day, the Prince Kamrān, having made a forced march of fifty miles from Zuffer, arrived, when a watch of the night had passed, in front of our encampment, where he drew up in battle array. As soon as the day broke, the King ordered his troops to form into line, and oppose the enemy.

When Kamrān saw our army drawn out, he made a violent charge, but was strenuously opposed by Hajy Muhammed Khān, who was posted on the left of the King, but who was obliged to give away. I have heard that on that occasion the Prince Kamrān with his own hand clove the skull of one of the Hajy's followers from the top of his head to the nose; in short, that division was routed, and Kamrān's followers having obtained much booty, retired with it to the fort of Talicān, of which they had previously gained possession. On hearing of this event, his Majesty enquired what they had done with the library, and was informed that it was quite safe.

In short, after the rout of our left division, the King, having ordered his own standard to be unfurled, and the kettle drums to be beaten, advanced in person against Kamrān, who being thereby terrified, made his retreat to Talicān. His Majesty then advanced close under the walls of the fort, and gave orders to put to death every follower of Kamrān that should be taken prisoner; but after several of them had been killed, he had compassion on the remainder, and let them go.

The King then encamped in a grove at a short distance from the fort, and wrote the following note to the Prince: "Oh, my unkind brother, what are "you doing? every murder that is committed on either side, you will be

" answerable for at the *Day of Judgement:* come, and make peace, that " mankind may be no longer oppressed by our contest." He then called a messenger, named Nesyb, the astrologer, and told him to carry the note to the Prince Kamrān. When the messenger came to the fort, and told his errand, he was allowed to enter, and he delivered the note. After the Prince had read it, he remained silent; on which Nesyb requested an answer: the Prince then repeated the following well known verse;

" He shall obtain the bride of the kingdom who embraces her across the edge of the sharp sword."

Nesyb then made his obeisance, came away, and reported the circumstance to his Majesty.

The King then gave orders to station the troops round the fort, and to erect batteries at several places, and on this occasion ordered me (the author) to erect one of them before he returned to that spot. His Majesty was employed the whole night in fixing the batteries, after which he gave orders for the guns to be mounted. For nearly two months a fire was kept up against the fortress; at length Kamrān being reduced to great extremities, made it known that if the King would send his Almoner into the fort, he might there proclaim him as the rightful sovereign.

In consequence of this information, on the first Friday, Mulānā Abd al Baky, the *Sudder*, went into the fort, and read the Khutbeh in his Majesty's name.

On the following day Carajā Khān, and the other chiefs who had deserted, came with quivers and swords tied about their necks, and threw themselves at his Majesty's feet, who was pleased to pardon them. On that night the Prince Kamrān made his escape from the fort, and halted on the bank of the river Bengy. Here he was attacked by the troops of Myrzā Ibrahīm Hussyn, son of Solimān, King of Badukhshan, and taken prisoner. On hearing this circumstance, his Majesty sent an agent to Hussyn to demand his prisoner; he also sent an honorary dress and several presents to Kamrān, all of which he respectfully received; and having put on the dress, agreed to wait on the King, who in the mean time took possession of Talicān.

CHAPTER XXIII.

Of the arrival of the Prince Kamrān, the division of the country, and of the King's return to Kabul. A. H. 955.—A. D. 1548.

When the King was informed of the intentions of Kamrān he was much pleased, and gave orders that the chains should be taken off Myrzā Askery, who had remained in confinement since the indisposition of his Majesty. When the Prince Kamrān approached, orders were given to all the chiefs to go out and meet him; tents were also pitched for his reception, and the bands of music stationed at the proper places to give notice of his arrival. On his first entering the camp, he was carried to the tent of Prince Hindal; but without giving him time to sit down, he was informed he might proceed to the tent of audience, as the King was ready to receive him. As soon as he stepped on the carpet of the royal pavilion, he took a handkerchief from one of the attendants and tied it round his own neck (as an acknowledgement of his crimes); his Majesty, on seeing this, said, "oh my dear brother, there is no necessity for this, throw off the handkerchief." The Prince then made three salutations, after which the King embraced him, and caused him to sit down on his right hand. After he had made some excuses the King arose, and said, "what has taken place was a ceremonious meeting, now let us meet as *brothers;*" they then reciprocally embraced each other: upon which the trumpets sounded, and the whole assembly were much delighted: a cup of sherbet was then brought, half of which was drank by the King, the other half by the Prince; they then entered into familiar conversation. After which the Princes Hindal and Askery were seated on the same carpet with them, and the four brothers eat *salt* together;* they then offered up prayers for his Majesty's prosperity. The feast was prolonged for two days, which were passed in every kind of rejoicing.

On the following day the King marched from Talicān, with his three brothers, to the fountains of *Ashek Meshek,* where they remained for a week; during which time the King made a division of the country between them

* This was considered as a renewal of their vows of friendship.

and the other chiefs. The districts of Kūlāb he assigned to the Princes Kamrān and Askery, burthened with a pension to Chaker Beg, one of the generals of Kamrān. The forts of Talicān and Zuffer, with their dependencies, were given to Myrzā Solimān, and that of Candahar to the Prince Hindal. After this division they all took the vow of fealty, and were dismissed to their respective governments; and the King, having first taken the fort of Purian, which belonged to the Syāhposhans, gave it in charge of Mulk Aly, and then returned to Kabul.

Some time after this it was reported to the King that a dispute had taken place between the Prince Kamrān and Chaker Beg; that the former had left the country of Kūlāb,* but had previously inflicted a severe chastisement on the latter. In consequence of this information, his Majesty sent Myrzā Shāh Sultān to reprimand Chaker Beg, but forwarded a letter to the Prince, inviting him to come to Kabul, and that he would bestow on him a more valuable district. The Myrzā went and delivered the letter, but the Prince said, "I have now abandoned the affairs of this world, and have no wish for any further employment in it." Although this was his verbal answer, his heart was still full of deceit, and he meditated some other schemes.

The King, ignorant of his brother's plans, resolved upon conquering the province of Balkh, with an intention of making it over to Kamrān. With this view he marched, accompanied by the Prince Hindal, Myrzā Solimān, and a number of other chiefs towards Balkh, expecting that his brother would join him on the route, but in this hope he was disappointed.

When the army reached the fort of *Aybek*, which was garrisoned by the troops of Pyr Khān, the Uzbeg chief, the King laid siege to it; in a few days took it; and having found there the family of the Prince Kamrān, sent them to Kabul: of the Uzbeg prisoners, some he released, and some of them he kept in the camp: one of the chiefs, named Atabeg Beg, he took into his own service, who strongly advised him not to proceed against Balkh, as he would thereby rouse the whole tribe of Uzbegs against him; but the King would not listen to his advice, and marched on. When the army arrived in the neighbourhood of Balkh, some of the Uzbegs came out of the fort, and

* There is a town called *Tūlāb*, mentioned in Baber's Memoirs, which I suspect is the same place.

engaged us, but in a short time were driven back. On this occasion the Prince Hindal followed them as far as the stone bridge, and sent a message to his Majesty, " that if he would support him, they might then take the city by storm;" but the King refused, saying, " he would attack the place next morning."

During the night intelligence was brought that the faithless Kamrān had made a sudden march with an intention of again surprising Kabul. On hearing of this news, the chiefs and soldiers, whose families had been left in that fortress, were quite dismayed, which circumstance compelled the King to retreat in great haste; and being pursued by the Uzbegs, we were thrown into great disorder, and the troops suffered exceedingly, but reached Kabul in time to avert Kamrān's evil intentions.*

CHAPTER XXIV.

Battle of Kipchāk, in which the King was severely wounded. A. H. 957.—A. D. 1550.

The King having again entered the city of Kabul remained there for three months, when intelligence was brought to him that the Prince Kamrān was still wandering about the country with bad intentions. His Majesty therefore having collected a few of his troops marched from Kabul. On the first day he halted at Carā Bāg; the next he proceeded to Charehkaran, and on the third reached the bank of the river Baran: he continued his march to the pass of Kipchāk, and came to a river, over which he swam his horse. On this occasion not one of the chiefs followed him, but went up the bank till they found a ford; on which his Majesty, being angry, said, " Oh ye blockheads! when Shāh Ismael of Persia threw his handkerchief down a precipice, twelve thousand of his followers immediately precipitated themselves after it, and were dashed to pieces: you have allowed me, your King, to pass the river alone, and not a single soldier has followed me; what good can I expect from such troops?"

The King then consulted with Carajā Khān what was next to be done:

* Here follows a long anecdote of Sultān Muhammed Ghiznevy, to evince the fickleness of fortune, but it is omitted in the Translation.

the Khān replied, " there are several passes in this part of the country; I advise your Majesty to secure them, by which means we may seize the Prince Kamrān, and put an end to all further commotion and disturbance."

In consequence of this advice the King sent off Hajy Muhammed, his foster brother, with a division of the army to secure the pass of *Syrtun*, while he with the remainder of the troops crossed the pass of Kipchāk, and encamped about a *coss* on the other side of it.

While in this situation, intelligence was brought that the Prince Kamrān was in the rear of his Majesty, and was forcing the pass. On this the King re-entered the pass, and in a few hours was opposed by the Prince: in a short time several of the loyal chiefs were cut down; the horse of Muhammed Amyn was also rendered unserviceable; but the King presented him with one of his own led horses, and said to him, " as I know your father is one of Kamrān's confidential followers, you had better go and join him;" Amyn replied, " I care not for my father; I will never quit your Majesty."

About this time one of the scoundrels of the enemy approached the King, and struck him on the head with his sword, and was about to repeat the blow, when his Majesty looking at him, said, " you *wretch!* how dare you?" upon which the fellow desisted, and some other officers coming up, led the King out of the battle; but he was so severely wounded, that he became weak from loss of blood, and therefore threw off his *Jubba*,* and gave it in charge of an Abyssinian servant; but the servant being obliged to make his escape from the battle, threw away the *Jubba*, which having been found by some of Kamrān's followers, it was brought to the Prince, who immediately proclaimed that the King was killed.

At this time there only remained with his Majesty eleven persons, including servants, and the author of these pages. We therefore took him out of the battle; and as his own horse was unquiet, we mounted him on a small ambling steed, two of the chiefs supporting him on either side, and endeavouring to console him by anecdotes of former Princes who had suffered similar adversity, and encouraged him to exert himself, as it was probable the enemy might pursue him. On hearing this, he resumed his fortitude,

* A coat, made of very strong quilted silk or cotton, used as armour: it will turn the sharpest sword, or a spent ball.

and proceeded towards the pass of *Syrtun.** On the march we were joined by some of the chiefs, and at nightfall reached the entrance of Syrtun. As it was then very cold, and his Majesty suffered much from weakness, a sheep-skin cloak was brought and put on him.

In the morning we reached the top of the pass; and as it was then getting warm, the King dismounted on the bank of the river, performed his ablutions, and washed his wound; but as there was no carpet for prayer to be found, the humble servant, *Jouher*, brought the cover of a stool of scarlet cloth, and spread it for his Majesty, who knelt thereon, and performed his devotions, and sat down facing the *Kibleh (Mecca)*.

While in this situation Sultān Muhammed came up, and having made his salutation, *walked round* the King, and said, "he was willing to offer his own life for the preservation of his Majesty's."

The King then enquired if he had any news of the other division of the army? he replied, "that Hajy Muhammed, with his division, was coming, and would very shortly join him: just as his Majesty had again mounted his horse the Hajy arrived, followed by three hundred well equipped cavalry, had the honour of paying his respects, and of congratulating the King on his narrow escape.

The King was at this time suspicious of Sultān Muhammed and some other chiefs; he therefore resolved upon returning to Kabul. After riding for some time, we arrived at Zohākmaran; his Majesty then dismounted under a tree, and calling for pen and ink, he wrote a letter to his family, explaining the circumstances of the battle, and his fortunate escape: several of the followers also wrote to their families. He then sent off the letters by Hajy Muhammed and Shāh Muhammed, with orders that as soon as they had delivered them at Kabul, they should proceed to Ghizneh, and secure that fortress against the attacks of the Prince Kamrān.

Having despatched these officers, the King again mounted, and rode on to Purwan, where he alighted. At this place the only tent that could be procured was a small *Shamianeh* (canopy), sufficient only to skreen one person; under this his Majesty lay down and slept. In the morning the author of these pages awoke his Majesty, and told him it was the hour of morning

* It is in the vicinity of Bamian, or *Alexandria.*

prayer. He said, "my boy, as I am so severely wounded, I cannot bear to purify myself with *cold* water;" I represented that I had got some *warm* water ready for him: he then arose, performed his ablutions, and said his prayers. He afterwards mounted his horse, but had not ridden far when he complained that the clotted blood on his clothes hurt him, and asked of the servants if they had no Jameh (coat) they could lend him: Behader Khān replied, "he had a Jameh, but it was one his Majesty had discarded and given to him, and he had worn it;" the King said, "never mind that, bring it:" he then put it on, and gave the dress which was stained with blood to his humble servant Jouher, the *Aftabchy*, and said, "take care of this dress, and only wear it on holy days."

From Purwan we proceeded to *Kehemrūd*, where Taher Muhammed had the honour of paying his respects; he had pitched an old tent for the King, and had prepared an entertainment for him; but the blockhead did not bring any present, not even a spare dress. His Majesty ordered his followers to partake of the dinner, but went himself to the edge of a fountain, where they pitched an old tent, grimed with smoke and soot, for him; but as there was no necessary tent, the humble servant went and procured two hurdles, which he fixed up as a privy. At this time an old woman came and offered his Majesty a pair of *silk trowsers*; he said, "although these are not proper for *a man* to wear, yet, as my own are defiled with blood, I will put them on." He then enquired what the woman had for her support; and on being informed, wrote an order to the Collector not to demand any tribute from her in future.

Intelligence was now brought that a caravan of three hundred horses had arrived; the King therefore ordered two of the chiefs to bring the horses to him to look at: they went and returned, saying, "there were seventeen hundred more horses come;" his Majesty said, "I will go and settle the business myself:" he then mounted, and having given orders to secure the end of the pass, which prevented the merchants from attempting to escape, they respectfully waited on the King, and the senior of them having presented a bow and nine arrows, offered up prayers for his success. After that the horses were valued, and his Majesty gave the owners his bond for the amount saying, "if it please God to give me the victory, I will immediately pay you."

The next day we marched to *Alenjek*, which was then the residence of one of the wandering tribes, and remained there for seven days, during which period the chief of the tribe daily presented his Majesty with sixty goats or sheep, and sixty skins of buttermilk, which was distributed among the followers: the King also gave one or more of the horses to each of them.

We then marched, and encamped on the banks of the river Bengy. Soon after we were halted, a person came and called out, "O, people of the caravan! can you give me any information respecting the King Humāyūn?" On hearing this, his Majesty desired that no answer should be given; but that they should enquire who he was, who had sent him, and what news he brought: the man replied, "that he was sent by Besal Alenky, of the tribe of Beshy; that it was reported there had been a battle between the King and the Prince Kamrān; that the former had been wounded, and compelled to retreat; that the King's *Jubba* had been found in the jungle, and had been brought to the Prince, who was thereby convinced that the King was no more."

His Majesty then ordered the man to be brought to him, and asked him, "do you know me?" the man replied, "yes, I do;" the King said, "go and give my compliments to Besal Alenky, and tell him, when I come back this way to wait on me."

About mid-day his Majesty said to Hajy Muhammed, his foster brother, "as we have a number of spare horses with us, I wish you to search for a ford; go, and when you have found it, return and take me with you." The aforesaid person went, and having found a ford, sent a message by his servant that he had done so, then crossed the river, and requested the King to follow; but as he did not return himself as he was ordered, his Majesty began to suspect that he also had deserted: he, however, mounted his horse, and seeing me, made a signal for me to follow him; after which we were joined by Allah Kuly Khān. Nearly a watch of the night had passed when we crossed the river, and were there met by Hajy Muhammed, and the remainder of the night was spent in conversation.

CHAPTER XXV.

Account of Myrzā Kamrān again getting possession of Kabul, and of the young Akber, &c.
A. H. 957.—A. D. 1551.

The next morning the King, having mounted his horse, rode to *Aulia Khenja:* here the Prince Hindal also arrived, paid his respects, and offered to the King all the insignia of nobility which he used; after which we again marched, and reached the fort of Anderab, where the King fixed his residence. We must now return to the affairs of the Prince Kamrān, who after the battle encamped at Charkerān; the next morning he made a long march, and appeared before Kabul. It must be recollected that when his Majesty left Kabul he bestowed the government on Casim Aly, who had formerly been a servant of Kamrān's; but, notwithstanding this circumstance, he for some time refused to give up the fortress, till assured by Kamrān that the King was dead, who in proof thereof produced the Jubba or coat of mail; in consequence of which the Prince was allowed to enter the fort, and again take possession of the young Akber. This news was brought to the King at Anderab, but he was at the same time comforted by the junction of Solimān Myrzā, of Badukhshan, and several other chiefs. After remaining a month and twenty days at Anderab, intelligence was brought that the Prince Kamrān had left Kabul, and had entered the mountains of Hindū Kūsh, and was laying the country waste. The King then determined on marching to oppose the rebels; but he first assembled all his chiefs, and proposed to them to take the oath of allegiance; Hajy Muhammed Khān said, " it was also incumbent on his Majesty to take the oath of confederacy;" the Prince Hindal said, " such a proceeding was highly improper;" but the King said, " if the chiefs wished it, he would take the oath to satisfy them." In short, the oaths were ratified on both sides; and to give the ceremony more solemnity, the King fasted all that day.

On Thursday the King marched from Anderab, and encamped on the skirts of the mountain Hindū Kūsh; the next day he marched to Penjchereh (now Penjsheher), thence to Shutergurden, where he found his brother Kamrān drawn up to oppose him.

The King, anxious to avoid bloodshed, called Shāh Sultān, and sent him with a message to the Prince, saying, " that the district of Kabul was not worthy of contending for; let us leave our families in the fort, and let us join and invade Hindūstān through the Lumghanāt." The Prince was inclined to accept these terms, but the scoundrel Carajā dissuaded him, saying, " we will rather be hung on the gates of Kabul than give it up." Shāh Sultān returned with a negative to his proposition, and gave information against Carajā.

On this the King called a council of all his chiefs, and deliberated on what were the measures most proper to be pursued. After the council broke up, his Majesty gave orders that the troops should next morning put on their armour, mount their horses, and proceed to engage the enemy: Myrzā Solimān commanded the right wing, and the Prince Hindal the left; the advance was led by Hajy Muhammed (the King's foster brother): but when the army arrived within a short distance of the rebels, Hajy Muhammed, who was suspected of intriguing with Kamrān, objected to engage on *that day*, and requested the King to postpone the contest till the following one.

His Majesty at first consented to this proposal, and gave orders for the army to halt, and encamp; but several of the other chiefs came up, and opposed this measure, saying, " the tents were a long way in the rear, that the day should not be lost, and we ought to engage." The King then agreed that, as soon as he had performed his usual prayers, they should advance.

CHAPTER XXVI.

Defeat of the Prince Kamrān, and the death of his counsellor Carajā Khān. A. H. 958.—A. D. 1551-2.

The army of Kamrān was drawn up on a high hill; but his Majesty having ordered his matchlock-men to open a fire on them, the scoundrel (carabukht) Carajā made a charge with his cavalry on our left wing, and threw them into disorder; he again charged our right wing, when by the decree " of the Almighty, the disposer of all events," a ball struck him, and he fell lifeless on the plain: some of our soldiers seeing the wretch fall, immediately galloped up, cut off his head, and brought it to the King, who said, "it should be hung on the gate of Kabul, to make good the words of the traitor." Soon after this the Prince Kamrān fled in great dismay, and was pursued by the Prince Hindal. The Myrzā Ibrahim was ordered immediately to proceed to Kabul, and Myrzā Solimān to remain with his Majesty; but the King marched the next day, and on the second day again entered Kabul in triumph. But previous to the King's entering the fortress, he was met by the young Prince Akber; his Majesty embraced the child, kissed his forehead and eyebrows, returned thanks to the Almighty for his favour, and, in fact, renewed the meeting of the *Patriarch Jacob and his son Joseph.*

After a short time intelligence was brought that the Prince Kamrān was still loitering between Kabul and the river Sind; his Majesty, therefore, marched in that direction; but when he arrived at Chekry was informed that the Prince had taken refuge with the Afghān chief, Muhammed Khelyl; he, therefore, resolved to push on to the territory of that chief. On arriving at a place called Cheperha, fearing the night attacks of the Afghāns, he gave orders to erect a redoubt, in order to defend the army against any sudden attack: having fixed on a spot for the fort, the people were employed in erecting it.

During this interval, while the King and his brother Hindal were returning to the camp, *three* deer passed by them, one of which was shot by Abu al Mualy, the second escaped, but the Prince transfixed with an arrow the third; it fell on its side, raised its large eyes to heaven, and expired: the attendants were astonished at its motions, and said, "this antelope appears to have laid its complaint before the *redresser of all wrongs*, may it turn out well!" the Prince then proceeded, and joined his Majesty.

The following night the Prince Kamrān induced the Afghāns to make an attack upon our camp: the King was in the redoubt; but the Prince Hindal was actually going the rounds of the camp, and keeping the people on the alert, when the assault commenced: having no other arms but the very *bow and arrow* with which he had shot the antelope, he opposed the enemy; but in the furious onset of the Afghāns he was soon cut down, and thus became a martyr in defence of his Majesty.

The Afghāns were, however, repelled; but when the affair was over, and his Majesty enquired for his brother Hindal, no person had the courage to reply. He then mounted the highest place of the ground, and called out the name of his brother; but, although surrounded by at least three hundred persons, no one answered. He then ordered Abdal Vehab to go and search for the Prince; the messenger went; but when returning was shot by one of our matchlock men, who took him for an Afghān; thus by mistake he was also added to the number of martyrs. After that Abdal Hy was sent, and brought back the melancholy intelligence.

On hearing it the King instantly retreated to his tent, where he was overwhelmed with grief, but the chiefs endeavoured to console him, by saying that the Prince was blessed and happy in having thus fallen a martyr in the service of his Majesty, for whose long life they joined in offering up their anxious prayers. From this place we marched, and took post in the fort of Bysut, but the Afghāns surrounded us on all sides; and whenever they caught hold of any of the Moghuls, plundered and put them to death; they even reproached us for not coming out to fight them.

CHAPTER XXVII.

Account of the defeat of the Afghāns—of the flight of Prince Kamrān—of his taking refuge with Sultān Adam, the Ghicker chief—of his being given up to the King, by whose orders he was blinded. A. H. 960-1.—A. D. 1552-3.

After we had been for some days pent up in the fort, our chiefs began to murmur at our want of exertion; on which the King ordered out some spies to bring intelligence of the situation of the enemy; they returned with information that the Afghān chiefs were enjoying themselves with their respective clans; that they had no fears from his Majesty, and that they had agreed that the Prince Kamrān should spend a week with each of the clans (cabyleh) in succession.

On hearing this report, his Majesty, *the Prince Akber*, and the general Abu al Mualy, perfumed their heads, bathed, and said their Friday prayers, to be prepared for death; and on the following morning, having mounted their horses, they sallied out with all their troops on the Afghāns, who although at least amounting to twelve thousand were shortly dispersed, and left an immense number of cattle and sheep in our hands, with some of their women and children; but the Prince Kamrān again made his escape, re-entered Hindūstān, and sought refuge with Selim (son and successor of the usurper Shyr Shāh).

After this victory the King returned to Kabul, made great rejoicings, and bestowed largesses on all the chiefs.

The following year (A.H. 962, A.D. 1554) his Majesty meditated the invasion of Hindūstān, and therefore took measures to secure the fortress of Candahar (against the Persians) previous to setting out. About this time the King received letters from Sultān Adam, chief of the Ghickers, stating, "that the Prince Kamrān was now in his territory, and that if his Majesty would take the trouble of coming there, he would give him up."

In consequence of this information the King immediately marched; and having entered the country of Bungish, first seized and put to death a pretended prophet, who was leading mankind astray by teaching them a false religion; after which he proceeded to Dhencūt (Deencote of the maps); he then crossed the Nilāb (Indus), and, after repeated marches, entered the territory of Sultān Adam. When arrived within ten coss of the residence of this chief, he was met by an ambassador, who requested him to proceed; he, therefore, about mid-day reached Pirhala:* his Majesty then ordered tents to be pitched for the meeting between him and the Prince Kamrān; but the ambassador returned, and said, "that the Prince insisted upon the King's coming further to meet him." On hearing this his Majesty was surprised, and said, "after I have taken the trouble of coming so far, and have prepared accommodation for the interview, it is strange that he should delay the visit;" but to gratify him the tents were sent on another stage. At this place the ambassador again returned, and said, "the Prince was not yet satisfied, and requested the King would still advance;" his Majesty replied, "after evening prayers I will do so."

About this time the Ghicker chief, Sultān Adam, attended by two others, came and paid their respects. The King said, "Sultān Adam, you have

* See Edinburgh Gazetteer.

taken a long time to perform this ceremony;" the Chief replied, "I should certainly have done myself the honour of waiting on your Majesty at the Nilāb, but I had a *guest* in my house, whom I could not leave (Kamrān);" the King replied, "you have done right, that was of more consequence."

Sultān Adam again repeated the Prince's request that the King would move on; his Majesty hesitated for some time; but the Chief said, "the Prince Kamrān is my prisoner; you may do as you like." On this the King advanced to the banks of the river (Rud Ab), and sat there on a bed or couch. After about an hour of the night had passed the Prince arrived, and advanced with great humility; the King, however, received him graciously, and pointed to him to sit down on the bed on his right hand; his Majesty then sat down on the bed also, having the young Prince Akber on his left hand; Sultān Adam, Abū al Mualy, and the other chiefs, were also seated in due order. After some time his Majesty called for a water melon, one-third of which he himself took, and divided it with his brother; another third he gave between Akber and Abū al Mualy, and the remaining third between Terdy Beg and Sultān Adam. After this the Prince Kamrān made an apology in the name of several other chiefs for not having waited on the King, but said they would do so next morning. His Majesty replied, "very well, let them do so;" but Sultān Adam said, "as your Majesty has taken the trouble of coming so far, it will be more respectful for them to wait on you immediately:" he, therefore, sent off a messenger for them; and the chiefs having been introduced, were graciously received. The King then enquired if the tents were all pitched; and being informed that they were, having first distributed *pawn* to all the visitors, he mounted his horse and rode to the encampment. Preparations having been made for an entertainment, and public singers assembled, the whole night was passed in jollity and carousing. Early in the morning, the King having said his prayers, lay down to rest; the Prince Kamrān retired to his own tent, and did the same. The next night was also passed in festivity.

On the following day the King's officers demanded of him what he meant to do with the Prince Kamrān? he replied, "let us first satisfy the Ghicker chief, after which I will do whatever is deemed proper."

On the third day a grand entertainment was expressly given to Sultān

Adam; he was clothed in a dress of honour; the standard, kettle-drums, and all other insignia of royalty were conferred upon him; after which he was graciously dismissed.

On the next day the business of Myrzā Kamrān was taken into consideration; and it was resolved in the first place to remove all his servants from him. Then the King ordered five of his own people, viz. Khenjer Beg, Arif Beg, Aly Dūst, Sydy Muhammed, and his humble servant Jouher, to attend upon the Prince; and he said to me, " my boy, do you know where you are sent?" I said, " yes; and I know your Majesty's (wishes):" he replied, " your business is to take care of the interior of the tent; you are desired not to sleep for a moment." In obedience to the King's orders, I waited on the Prince about the hour of the second prayer; he asked for a carpet, for the purpose of kneeling on: I brought one, and spread it for him. In the evening he performed his devotions inside the tent. After that, he said, " boy,* what is your name?" I replied, " my name is Jouher;" he asked, " do you know the art of *champooing* (khademy)?" I replied, " yes, a little;" I then began to champoo him. He asked, " how long have you been in the King's service?" I replied, " I have been nineteen years in his Majesty's employ;" he said, " you are an old servant;" I replied, " yes:" he then asked me, " if I had ever been in the service of the Prince Askery;" I answered, " no:" he then said, " I have fasted six days, during this holy month of Ramzān; can you be my deputy for the remainder of the month?" I replied, " I can, but your highness will do it yourself; keep up your courage; do not allow melancholy anticipations to take possession of your heart:" he then said, " do you think they will kill me?" I replied, " princes only understand the motives or intentions of princes; but this I am certain of, that no man should commit suicide; and I know that his Majesty is a very compassionate personage." The night passed in this kind of melancholy discourse.

Early in the morning the King marched towards Hindūstān, but before his departure determined that the Prince should be blinded, and gave orders accordingly; but the attendants on the Prince disputed among themselves who was to perform the cruel act. Sultān Aly, the paymaster, ordered Aly

* The word *ghulam*, may be rendered either slave or boy.

Dūst to do it; the other replied, "you will not pay a Shāh Rukhy (3*s.* 6*d.*) to any person without the King's directions; therefore, why should I commit this deed without a personal order from his Majesty? perhaps to-morrow the King may say, 'why did you put out the eyes of my brother?' what answer could I give? depend upon it I will not do it by *your order.*" Thus they continued to quarrel for some time: at length, I said, "I will go and inform the King." On which I, with two others, galloped after his Majesty: when we came up with him, Aly Dūst said, in the *Jagtay Tūrky* language, "no one will perform the business." The King replied in the same language, abused him, and said, "why don't you do it yourself?"

After receiving this command, we returned to the Prince, and Ghulam Aly represented to him in a respectful and a condoling manner that he had received positive orders to blind him; the Prince replied, "I would rather you would at once *kill me;*" Ghulam Aly said, "we dare not exceed our orders:" he then twisted a handkerchief up as a ball for thrusting into the mouth, and he with the *Ferash* seizing the Prince by the hands, pulled him out of the tent, laid him down and thrust a lancet (Neshter) into his eyes (such was the will of God). This they repeated at least fifty times; but he bore the torture in a manly manner, and did not utter a single groan, except when one of the men who was sitting on his knees pressed him; he then said, "why do you sit upon my knees? what is the use of adding to my pain?" This was all he said, and acted with great courage, till they squeezed some (lemon) juice and salt into the sockets of his eyes; he then could not forbear, and called out, "O Lord, O Lord, my God, whatever sins I may have committed have been amply punished in this world, have compassion on me in the next."*

After some time he was placed on horseback, and we proceeded to a *grove* planted by the Emperor Firoz Shāh, where, it being very hot, we alighted; and after a short period again mounted, and arrived in the camp, when the Prince was lodged in the tent of Myr Cassim.

The Author of these pages seeing the Prince in such pain and distress,

* The usual mode of blinding Princes was, by passing a hot *Myl* (needle or bodkin) over the pupil of the eye, which did not give much pain. Ferishta and Abul Fazil both erroneously state that it was done by antimony.

could no longer remain with him; I therefore went to my own tent, and sat down in a very melancholy mood: the King having seen me, sent Jān Muhammed, the librarian, to ask me "if the business I had been employed on was finished, and why I had returned without orders?" the humble servant represented, "that the business I had been sent on was *quite completed;*" his Majesty then said, "he need not go back, let him get the water ready for me to bathe."

The next day we marched, and entered the territory of the chief, *Piraneh Januah.* The aforesaid Piraneh came and paid his respects to the King; but Sultān Adam having requested that the country might be given to him, it was so; his Majesty then entered the country of Rajā Sunker, plundered about fifty of the villages, and took a number of captives; but these were released upon paying a certain ransom, by which the army gained considerable wealth.

The King now resolved on going to Cashmire; but the chiefs said, "this is not a proper season for going to such a country as Cashmire;" the King was, however, obstinate, and Abū al Mualy shot one of the refractory Moghul chiefs with an arrow, and ordered the others to march; on which several of the nobles seeing the determination of his Majesty, went and complained to to Sultān Adam, who immediately came to the King, and falling at his feet, requested him to forego his intention, assuring him that Islam Khān *Sūr** was advancing into the Punjāb, and that the Afghāns, who had for some time abandoned the fort of Rhotas and crossed the Behut river, had returned and again taken possession of that district; he, therefore, advised his Majesty to return for the present to Kabul and Candahar, and having there recruited his army, he might next year come back and enter Hindūstān or Cashmire; but in the mean time to place the river Sind between him and his enemies, and trust to Providence for the furtherance of his wishes.

* Sultān Selim.

CHAPTER XXVIII.

Return of the King to Kabul, and of his granting permission to the Prince Kamrān to proceed on a pilgrimage to Mecca, &c. A. H. 961.—A. D. 1553.

Sultān Adam having represented to his Majesty that the inhabitants of that part of the country were suffering much from the presence of his army, requested that he would issue orders for them to march immediately to the westward. In consequence of this representation, the public crier* was sent round to proclaim the orders, and we accordingly marched to the banks of the Nilāb. At this place the King gave permission for the Prince Kamrān to proceed (by way of Tattah) to the pilgrimage of Mecca:† after which we crossed the river, and having reached Pyshavur, the King gave orders for erecting a fortress at that place; and although the chiefs grumbled at keeping the army longer in the field, his Majesty persevered, and the foundation of the fortress having been marked out that very day, it was finished in a week; and as the grain was still standing in the fields, he ordered it to be cut down and stored in the fort. The *Khutbeh* was then read in due form, and the command of the place was given to Sekunder Khān, an Uzbeg, and a dress of honour conferred on him.

After the second prayers the army again marched, and his Majesty soon after happily arrived at Kabul: he took up his residence in the upper fort, and passed the new year's day in great festivity and rejoicing.

Some time after this the King marched to Candahar, and remained there for three months; he then returned towards Kabul; Byram Khān accompanied him as far as the river Turung, which is half way between Ghizneh and Candahar, and then returned to his garrison; but previous to his departure it was settled that, as soon as the winter should be over, he would come to Kabul, and from thence attend his Majesty on the invasion of India.

About this period Hajy Muhammed (the foster brother) who commanded in Ghizneh was dissatisfied; and, although the King took measures to recon-

* The mode of issuing orders by the Orientals.

† He died near Mecca, A. H. 964. A. D. 1557.

cile him he was not contented, and a coldness continued between them; but when his Majesty made an excursion through the Lungham district, the Hajy broke the kettle-drums, standards, and other insignia of nobility which had been conferred on him, as a proof of his disrespect. On hearing this, the King sent and confined the Hajy and his brother, Shāh Muhammed, and said to them, with great temper, "do you write out a list of all your *merits*, and I will write your *demerits*, and let us see which preponderate; if your claims on me are more weighty than your transgressions against me, I will forgive you; but, if the contrary, I will not only dismiss you from my service, but put you to death." In short, they made out a list of their claims on the King, and he wrote an account of their faults; and, as the latter predominated, he ordered them both first to be confined, and afterwards to be slain.

His Majesty then returned to Kabul, but frequently went to amuse himself in hawking and fishing on the river Baran and in other places with his companions. During this period he sent letters to Samerkund, Bokhara, and other towns, inviting the chiefs and warriors to accompany him on his invasion of Hindūstān: to some of the chiefs he sent presents, and letters explanatory of his intentions, with prayers for their combined success.

CHAPTER XXIX.

Account of the King's invasion of Hindūstān, and of his regaining that empire. A. H. 962.—A. D. 1554-5.

Verse.

"O, wise man! the sphere of fortune is always revolving: it is constantly interchanging grief and happiness. Pleasure does not endure for ever, neither does pain continue to the end of time."

When every thing was arranged for the King's departure he quitted Kabul, and marched to Jellalabad; he there embarked on a raft,* and was pleasantly floated down the river to Pyshavur. Here he halted for two days, and sent off an express to Sultān Adam, the Ghicker chief, informing him of

* These rafts are frequently mentioned in Baber's Memoirs: they were composed either of timber and reeds, or of the latter supported on skins distended by air: they are called *Jalehs*.

his proceedings and further intentions. After that, by repeated marches the royal army reached the western bank of the Nilāb (Indus). It was on the last day of the month when the army crossed the river; and just as his Majesty passed over, *I, the humble servant*, saw the *new moon*, and immediately congratulated his Majesty on this auspicious event; also of his having crossed the river, and having re-entered the kingdom of Hindūstān at the moment of the new moon's appearance; the King replied, "God be praised, may it be propitious!" This he repeated three times. Amen.

After the troops had all passed the river, we continued our march day after day till we entered the district of Pirhala. At this place his Majesty said to his *humble servant*, "go, and have the Prince Akber bathed and dressed, and bring him hither." In obedience to the royal order, I went and delivered the message to the Prince, who said, "I cannot bathe, nor appear naked before you."* I replied, "if your Royal Highness pleases, I will call your *valet*, Refyk;" he said, "call him." After having bathed (in private) he put on a new dress, and I accompanied him to the King. When we arrived his Majesty was sitting, facing the setting moon; he ordered the Prince to sit down opposite him; he then read some verses of the Korān, and at the end of each verse *breathed* on the Prince, and was so delighted and happy, it might be said that he had then acquired all the good fortune of this world, and the blessings of the next. His Majesty then continued his journey, and when we arrived at the distance of four *coss* from the Pirhalā, he alighted.

The next day the King gave an order for a mustering of every description of his followers, and said he would commence with the *Ewry* department. In compliance with this order the humble servant Jouher, and the other persons belonging to the department, having dressed and armed ourselves, stood in a rank before the King, who having looked at us was much pleased, and said, "I consider this review as an auspicious omen;" on which, we all offered up prayers for his Majesty's success and happiness. Amen, Amen.

We then marched towards the river Chunāb; and when we had arrived within four coss of its bank, we came to a hill or high ground, on which the

* The Muhammedans are *very* scrupulous on this head, and some extraordinary anecdotes are related of them in consequence. The Prince was then thirteen years of age.

King directed his tents to be pitched, and the dinner to be served. After dinner he ordered the Khān Khanān, Byram Khān, and some other chiefs with their troops to proceed towards Jallindhar, and ascertain whether the Afghāns were still in these districts; if they were found, the chiefs were to return and inform his Majesty; but if not, they were to push on, cross the river Sutlege, and enter the district of Sirhind. His Majesty at the same time directed his secretary, his chamberlain, and several of the domestics to proceed to Lahore, and make preparations for his arrival in that city. On this, a servant named *Herbay*, came and said, "that Lahore was his birthplace, that all his family were there, and that if his Majesty would grant him permission, he would go on and make inquiries respecting them;" the King replied, "if you go, who is to carry my water bottle?" the paymaster and the chief eunuch replied, "his brother, Futteh Allah, will carry the bottle." His Majesty did not approve this arrangement, but said, "*he* may go, but I will give the bottle to another person:" he then ordered me to take charge of it.

The aforesaid Herbay having gone some distance, said to himself, "if the bottle is once given in charge to another attendant, God knows whether I shall ever get it back again."* Having thus reflected, he repented of what he had done, and during the night returned; but as the bottle had been entrusted to me, I thought it requisite to ask the King's permission before I gave it up. I therefore said to his Majesty, "is it your royal pleasure, that I shall continue in the *Abdar Khaneh* (water house), or in the *Ewry?*" he replied, "you are to remain in the latter, but remember you are always to keep a china cup, a jug with a lid, and the water bottle in your own possession; you are not to allow any other person to offer me water to drink without your seal being affixed; don't permit the bottle to remain empty during the night; when you give me to drink, pour the water into the china cup, and on the march have the bottle on the horse with you." Thus his Majesty kindly instructed me; but, as mankind is ever liable to error, the next morning, when we were about to march, Herbay having returned, asked me for the bottle, and I gave it to him; when we were all mounted, and the

* It may be unnecessary to add, that the office of bottle carrier is a very confidential situation: the bottle is made of leather, and called *Keruty*.

King saw the bottle in the hands of Herbay, he was very angry, and when he alighted gave me two blows on the side of the head, and said, "whenever I again confer an employment on you, beware not to resign it to any body." With this reprimand he graciously forgave me.

The chiefs that had been sent towards Jallindhar having crossed the Sutlege, and passed through Machwareh, entered the district of Sirhind, where they plundered all the property of the Afghān chief, Tatar Khān. The King in the mean time having arrived at Kullanur (Callanore of the maps), halted there for some days; during which time his Majesty and Abū al Mualy agreed to enter the northern range of hills; the chiefs, however, were not satisfied to do so, but being afraid to tell their opinion to the King, they employed me (Jouher) to explain to him, that it was highly impolitic to lose time by making excursions, when more important business was in hand. I did so; but concluded by saying, "they were willing to obey his orders;" the King replied, "very well, I will go back to Lahore." The order was immediately given, and we set out for that city.

When the King arrived within ten *coss* of Lahore, all the Syeds and principal people of the city, led by Shykh Abd Allah, came out to meet his Majesty; but as there were two parties in the place, headed by Mukhdum-al-Mulk and Myan-Hajy-Mehdy (religious persons), he had some difficulty in reconciling them.

The King then entered the city in state, and a few days afterwards made a division of the appointments of the province among his followers: to the humble servant *Jouher* was assigned the collection of the Pergunnah of Hybetpūr; but previous to my departure his Majesty called me, and said, "young man, listen to this story as a piece of advice." A *Moghul* having received an appointment,* began his supposed duty by snatching a blanket from the shoulders of a citizen, and upon the man's remonstrating, said, "you scoundrel, don't you know that I have been sent by Government to collect." On receiving this hint, I said, "I am aware of my own unfitness for public employment, but trust that through your Majesty's favour, and having had the honour for so many years of pouring water on the royal hands, I shall not discredit the appointment to which I have been nominated;"

* The Moghuls are made the butts of numerous anecdotes.

the King replied, "good produces good, and evil causes evil." I then made my obeisance.

When arrived in the Pergunnah, I found that it had been the custom of the Afghān farmers to give their wives or children in pledge to the *Hindū* bankers for money advanced on account of the collections; therefore, the first thing I did was to collect all the grain that had been hidden in dry wells and other places, and having sold it, paid the bankers, and liberated the families of the peasants. On hearing of this affair his Majesty was much pleased, and promoted me to the collectorship of the villages belonging to the Afghān chief, Tatar Khān Lody.*

CHAPTER XXX.

Of the battle between Omer Khān† Ghicker and the imperial general Abū al Mualy. A. H. 962.—A. D. 1555.

Information having been brought to the King that Omer Khān Ghicker having collected a very large force at Fyruzpūr, which is situated at the junction of the Beyah and Sutlege rivers, with an intention of joining the Afghān Emperor Sekunder, his Majesty called a council of his officers, in which it was determined to attack the Ghickers. In consequence of this resolution, a detachment under the command of Shāh Abū al Mualy was sent against them. The contending parties met in the Pergunnah of Chuhy: the enemy were about twelve thousand in number, while the royal forces consisted only of eight hundred cavalry, and a very furious battle took place; the Afghān general charged with such impetuosity on Abū al Mualy, that he nearly fell from his horse, and would have been slain, were it not that a brave Moghul soldier having placed a small drum on his head instead of a helmet, called out the war cry *Allah Akber* (God is greatest), and rushed on Omer Khān with such violence as to unhorse him; on seeing which the Afghāns took to flight. This was his Majesty's *first* victory since his re-entering Hindūstān, and if the disproportion of the numbers is taken into

* Abul Fazil mentions his appointment. See Price's Muhammedan History, vol. iii. page 923.

† By other historians he is called Shāh baz Khān.

‡ See Dow's Hindostan, vol. ii. page 197.

account, it will be evident that we were indebted to the grace of God for our success.

When the letters announcing this victory were received, his Majesty answered them, with hearty thanks to the army, and a promise of promotion to all who had distinguished themselves on the occasion; he also ordered that all the Afghān prisoners should be collected, and sent to him; but a chief, named Ferhad Khān, having represented to his Majesty that he had promised not to detain any prisoners, he commanded that they should all be released.

CHAPTER XXXI.

An account of the victory gained by the royal army at Machwareh.
A. H. 962.—A. D. 1555.

Soon after this time letters were received from the Khān Khānan, Byram Khān, then at Sirhind, stating that the enemy who had at first retreated were now advancing in very great force against him, under the command of the Afghān generals, Tatar Khān and Hybet Khān, and requested orders for his conduct: his Majesty replied, " have you not heard that my young general, Shāh Abū al Mualy, with only eight hundred horse, has defeated twelve thousand of the enemy, why should you ask for further orders? do as he did." On receipt of this reprimand, all the chiefs resolved to exert themselves to the utmost.

About this time the Afghāns, being puffed up with pride and self-sufficiency, marked out a ford across the Sutlege, opposite to the town of Machwareh, with an intention of crossing the river and of annihilating our small army; but Byram Khān, trusting in the divine protection, and the good fortune of his Majesty, crossed the river by the very ford the Afghāns had marked out, and the enemy having in their retreat set fire to some villages enabled our troops by the light of the fires to pierce them with our arrows: thus by the grace of God we obtained a *second* victory.

After this success our army advanced to Sirhind; from thence the Khān Khānan sent letters to inform his Majesty that Sultān Sekunder, the Afghān emperor, was advancing with an army of eighty thousand horse, while his forces amounted only to seven or eight hundred. As it was impossible for him to contend against so great a superiority, he requested the King would advance to his assistance, or allow him to retreat and form a junction. On receipt of these letters his Majesty wrote, "be patient only for two days, and I will join you." Accordingly the King crossed the Sutlege at Machwareh, and on the next day joined the army at Sirhind.

The Afghān Emperor advanced at the same time, and encamped opposite our army; he then said to his courtiers, what presumption it is in the King Humāyūn to oppose our army of eighty thousand horse with only five thousand!"

It now becomes requisite to mention an event in which I was personally concerned. It has been stated, that when the King took possession of Lahore, he appointed collectors to each of the districts of that province: thus when our army had crossed the river Sutlege, we were left without any military support; in consequence of which a body of four hundred Afghāns entered the province of Lahore, and began to plunder all around. When this intelligence reached the collectors,* we consulted together on what was to be done. I advised that we should assemble every man bearing arms that we could, and trusting to the good fortune of his Majesty and the Divine favour, advance against the plunderers. This measure being agreed to, we appointed Jellal Sunbuly, a brave and active young man, to lead our advanced guard, and having assembled about four hundred men, we crossed the river Zengy-sar during the night; and at the dawn of day having taken the Afghāns by surprise, and led on by the gāllant Jellal Sunbuly, we made a vigorous attack on them, and through the good fortune of his Majesty, completely defeated them, and took five of their chiefs prisoners.

We then wrote an account of these transactions to the King, and said, "your slaves have gained a victory over the enemy, and hope it will be a harbinger of your Majesty's conquest of the Afghān Emperor;" in answer to this letter we received a most gracious firman, approving our conduct, and desiring us to keep the prisoners till the end of the war, when their fate should be decided.

* Abul Fazil states that Ferhad Khān was appointed Foujdar (military governor) of the Penjāb, Baboos Beg Amyn (superintendant of the revenue), and *Mehter Jouher* (treasurer).

CHAPTER XXXII.

Of the victory gained by the King at Sirhind,* and the flight of the Afghān Emperor, Sekunder Sūr. A. H. 962.—A. D. 1555.

The contending armies having continued for nearly a month encamped opposite each other, his Majesty said, "we must employ the same means against the Afghān Emperor that I did against Sultān Behader of Gujerāt, that is, to cut off his supplies of grain and other provisions." In consequence of this determination, Terdy Beg Khān was ordered with his division to effect this measure. He accordingly marched, and having fallen in with a brother of the Emperor Sekunder Sūr, slew him, took all his insignia of nobility, and sent them to his Majesty.

After this event the two armies drew up opposite each other; his Majesty retained the command of one division, the second division was led by the Khān Khānan (Lord of Lords), the third by Shāh Abū al Mualy, and the fourth by Sekunder Khān, the Uzbeg. The Afghān Emperor considering that the strongest part of our line was that commanded by the Khān Khānan, made a furious attack upon it; but the Khān having thrown up an entrenchment in his front, merely stood on the defensive. During this time his Majesty was employed in prayer, and a report having been brought that the Khān Khānan was killed, he sent off a special messenger to ascertain the truth; and when informed that the report was groundless, returned thanks to God for it. He then ordered Shāh Abū al Mualy and Terdy Beg to wheel round the Afghāns and make an attack on their rear, while they were engaged in front. By the favour of the Almighty, who in a moment can convert a beggar to a king, and change a king into a beggar, and his Majesty's good fortune, this manœuvre was skilfully executed, and in a short time the Afghān army took to flight, and his Majesty obtained a decisive victory.

(Here follow a number of verses from the poet Nekhsheby.)

After this victory his Majesty proceeded towards Dehly; but it having

* See Edinburgh Gazetteer.

been ascertained that the Emperor Sekunder had taken refuge in the northern hills of the Penjāb, orders were given to Shāh Abū al Mualy to march to Jallindher and watch the motions of the fugitive; but the aforesaid chief not content with literally obeying his orders, afterwards proceeded to Lahore, where he took upon himself the command of the province, thereby superseding the officers left in charge by his Majesty.*

As I had received positive orders from the King to procure intelligence of every thing that was going on, even as far distant as Candahar and Kabul, I therefore sent spies into the camp of the Afghān Emperor, who brought me information that Sekunder having seized upon all the treasure he could find, was recruiting his army by employing a number of archers, and every idle person he could collect, and was encamped in the vicinity of the fortress of Mankūt. I, therefore, communicated this information to Shāh Abū al Mualy, who having consulted with his chiefs, resolved on marching against the Afghāns.

But, as I was aware of the inferiority of our numbers, I conjured the chiefs not to think of moving until provided with (Arabeh) carriages: they listened to my advice, and I immediately ordered a quantity of timber which had been brought for repairing the fort to be sawn up, and made into coarse carriages; I further said, here are a number of old chains will answer for some of the hooks and links, the remainder may be made of raw leather, which in fact is better for fastening the carriages together than iron: in short, we made a number of these carriages sufficient to surround the troops, and prevent the enemy from charging on them. Then the humble servant Jouher, in order to forward his Majesty's service, procured 300 *bows,* 300 quivers full of arrows, 300 spears, 250 shields, 50 *maunds* of gunpowder, and 30 *maunds* of lead for bullets. I also presented the General Abū al Mualy with a coat of mail, and other equipments, with all of which he was much pleased, and spoke very highly of my useful exertions; he even said, "I did not suppose that you had been a person of so much ability; whenever I shall see the King, I will not fail to recommend you in the strongest manner." He then distributed the above-mentioned articles to such of the troops as required them.

* Abul Fazil says that Abū al Mualy was appointed Governor of the Penjāb.

About this time nearly five hundred Moghul soldiers came from beyond the river Oxus to seek for employment; but as very few of them were armed, the General consulted me what he should do with them; I said, "give each of them a bow and a quiver of arrows, and advance them a small sum of money to support them for a month, by which time the business with the Afghāns will be settled." He took my advice, and having advanced the money to the Moghuls, they joined the army as volunteers.

After this the General advanced by easy marches towards the Emperor Sekunder, and every night surrounded his camp, with the *carriages* chained or tied together with leathern ropes, or with entrenchments.

It so happened, that during Abū al Mualy's residence at Lahore, he had frequently talked in a very presumptuous and independent manner, which raised suspicions against him, of which the officers in charge of the district thought proper to acquaint the King, and advised him either to return in person, or to nominate some other General to the command. In pursuance of this information his Majesty immediately appointed the Prince Muhammed Akber* and Byram Khān to command the army against the Emperor Sekunder; in consequence of which, upon their arrival at Sirhind, a number of the chiefs quitted Abū al Mualy's army and joined the Prince, which of course put an end to the General's operations against Sekunder, and his own ambitious projects. Abū al Mualy therefore wrote a complaint against these chiefs to the King, in which he mentioned that he had reduced the Afghān Emperor to great straits, and should certainly have captured him, had not the chiefs before mentioned deserted him. He at the same time sent an Arzy (representation) to the Prince and Byram Khān, stating his grievances, and urging them to advance and finish the business, as the enemy were now cooped up at the foot of the hills, but that *he* should leave the army and return to Lahore.† Byram Khān also informed his Majesty of all these particulars, said he would immediately proceed with the army to the Penjāb, but should order Abū al Mualy to return to the royal presence. Having obtained copies of the King's answers to these petitions, I subjoin them.

* See Price's Muhammedan History, vol. iii. page 933.

† In answer to this letter, the Prince and Byram Khān wrote to him a joint letter, viz. "Your

To Abū al Mualy he wrote:

"The representation of that fortunate *son* was duly received, and what "you wrote respecting the misconduct of certain chiefs was understood. "Please God, when they rejoin me, I will order their conduct to be inquired "into, and punish them according to their deserts; do you return to me "immediately."

To the Khān Khānan he wrote:

"Be it known to my faithful Generalissimo Byram Khān, Khān Khānan, "that letters have been received from our (adopted) son Abū al Mualy,* "stating that he had cleared the country of the enemy; why don't you ad-"vance more quickly to his assistance?"

On the very day that Abū al Mualy received the King's letter, an ambassador (Aylchy) of the Khān Khānan arrived at Lahore, and said to the General, "you have come here without any good reason, you must proceed immediately to the King;" the General replied, "I will set off instantly; call the other chiefs who came with me." Ishmael Sultān said, "*we* have marched fourteen *coss* this morning, and are much tired; besides, it is now evening, and heavy rain is coming on; if approved, we will set off early in the morning." This being agreed on, they consulted who was to entertain the Khān Khānan's ambassador, and determined that *Jouher* was the proper person, as being one of the officers of Lahore. In consequence, I took the agent to my house, and entertained him in a most hospitable manner. The next morning, accompanied by Abū al Mualy and the other chiefs, he set off to join his Majesty.

"letter safely arrived, and its contents were understood; do you come quickly here, after which "you must proceed and join his Majesty. *We* will very shortly enter that country."

* He was a Syed, and a great favourite of the King's.

CHAPTER XXXIII.

Account of the death of his Majesty, who now dwells in Paradise, and the ascending the Throne by his Majesty Jellal addyn Akber. A. H. 963.—A. D. 1556.

When Shāh Abū al Mualy quitted Lahore, he only marched the first day as far as the King's palace, there he halted for two days; he then proceeded and reached Calanore, where he was met by the Prince Akber and the Khān Khānan, attended by a number of chiefs, and reciprocal visits were interchanged, and a reconciliation took place; but while the armies were encamped here, the melancholy intelligence arrived that the King Humāyūn had drunk of the last cup from the hands of the Angel of Death.

[Quotation from the Korān.]

"Every soul shall taste of death; death is decreed to every man; and when it arrives, he can neither hasten it, nor delay it a single hour. From God we came, and to him we must return."

This event happened at Dehly on the 11th of the month Rubby al Avul, A. H. 963, January 21st, A.D. 1556.*

(Here follow a number of Persian verses; then a long dream of the Author portending this melancholy event.)

* The circumstances of the King's death are thus related in Dow's History of Hindostan, vol. ii. page 113.

"In the evening of the 7th of the first Rubby, Humāyūn walked out upon the terrace of the library, and sat down there for some time to enjoy the fresh air. When the Emperor began to descend the steps of the stair from the terrace, the crier, according to custom, proclaimed the time of prayer. The King, conformably to the practice of religion, stood still upon this occasion and repeated his creed, then sat down upon the second stair till the proclamation was ended. When he was going to rise, he supported himself on a staff, which unfortunately slipped upon the marble, and the King fell headlong from the top to the bottom of the stair: he was taken up insensible, and laid upon his bed; he soon recovered his speech, and the physicians administered all their art, but in vain; for upon the 11th of the month, about sun-set, his soul took her flight to Paradise. He was buried in the new city upon the banks of the river, and a noble tomb was

He concludes with prayers that the whole habitable world may be subjected to the *descendants* of the great Emperor Timūr, *Saheb Keran*, and *be* dependent on the kingdom of Dehly for ever.

He hopes that the liberal and enlightened persons of the age will excuse and pardon the imperfections and errors of his work, and prays that the readers of it may be preserved from all misfortunes.

Copied by Nazir, son of Talib Husseyny, in the month of Jemad al Avul, of the year of the reign 19. (Name omitted.)

erected over him some years after by his son Akber. Humāyūn died at the age of fifty-one, after a reign of twenty-five years in Kabul and India." *

On the 3rd of the second Rubby, A. H. 963, A. D. 1556, the illustrious Akber ascended the throne at the town of Calanore (Kullanūr) in the Penjāb, then in the fourteenth year of his age. Price's Muhammedan History, vol. iii. page 950.

---

* In the Memoirs of Baber it is stated that Humāyūn was born on the fourth day of (the eleventh month) Zilkād of A. H. 913, or January, 1508; and as he died on the seventh of (the third month) Rubby, A. H. 963, or January 1556, he was only forty-eight *solar* years of age, being nearly fifty *lunar* years.

APPENDIX TO CHAPTER XVI.—Page 77.

As very little of the history of Shāh Tahmāsp is generally known, I have, by permission of the Committee of the Oriental Translation Fund, reprinted the English part of a chapter of the *Aālem Arāy Abbassy*, published by me as an Appendix to the Descriptive Catalogue of the Library of Tippoo Sultān of Mysore in the year 1809, (now out of print,) as throwing a considerable light on the reign of that Persian monarch.

No. XXVI.—History.

Tarikh Aālum Arāy Abbassy.

Book I. contains the genealogy of the Persian kings of the Seffy dynasty, traced to Aly, the son-in-law of Muhammed; and the history of Shāh Ismael, the first monarch of that race, who commenced his reign, A. D. 1499; also the Life of his son Shāh Tahmāsp, with memoirs of the learned and other illustrious men who flourished during their reigns.

Book II. The History of Persia from the death of Shāh Tahmāsp in 1575 to the accession of Shāh Abbās.

Book III. Memoirs of the first thirty-three years of the reign of Shāh Abbās the Great, who ruled Persia with an iron hand for forty-five years.

Author, Sekunder Humnēshyny (the companion, A.D. 1616) dedicated to Shāh Abbās.

*An Account of the Arrival of Ambassadors from different Monarchs, at the Foot of the Imperial Throne of Shāh Tahmāsp.**

When his Majesty, who now resides in Paradise, had settled all the internal commotions of his kingdom, and had concluded a permanent peace with all

* This Prince was the second Persian monarch of the Sofy dynasty. He succeeded his father Ismail, A.D. 1523, and reigned with considerable reputation for fifty-two years. He was

his neighbours, he resided tranquilly for twenty years at the royal city of Cazvīn, without ever moving to any (considerable) distance from it.

During the whole period in which the royal throne was adorned by his Majesty's presence, the standards of his prosperity daily rose higher, and the eagle of his good fortune at length ascended to the sky. Various kings sent eloquent ambassadors to his court, entrusted with costly presents and valuable curiosities, as offerings to his Majesty. Of the most potent sovereigns of the world, and rulers of independent kingdoms, who frequently sent embassies to his Majesty, the first was, the chief of the Emperors of the age, the greatest of the kings of the dynasty of Othmān, the Sovereign of Rūm, Soleymān the Magnificent,* who, after being engaged for many years in war with his Majesty, sent the most confidential and principal of his ministers, Mohammed Pāshā, with letters, to solicit peace. In return for which compliment, Mīr Shems Addeen Khān was sent with an embassy from Persia; to whom the Emperor Soleymān was pleased to say, "From the commencement of the prosperity of the house of Othmān to the present moment, although kings from all quarters of the world have sent ambassadors to us, we have never (before) sent an embassy to any one, nor have we ever done more than merely sent a messenger with letters from our ministers." And, in fact, it never had been customary with the Othmāns to send ambassadors, until Sinān Beg, one of the chief confidants (of Soleymān), who, being taken prisoner by the Persians, and afterwards released, as we have before related, was sent, on the conclusion of peace between the two Empires, by Sultān Soleymān, to demand the Turkish Prince, Sultān Bāyezīd.† This ambassador arrived at the Gate of Paradise, Cazvīn, A. H. 966, (A. D. 1558); when, having obtained the honour of an audience, he assured his Majesty of the friendship of his master, and stated the objects of his embassy. During the

contemporary with the Othmān Sulṭān Soleymān, and the Emperor Homayun of Hindustan. With the former he had frequent wars, and enabled the latter to recover his kingdom from the usurper Shir Shāh. Our histories are very deficient in the accounts of this reign. Vide Universal History, Vol. V.

* Vide Universal History, Vol. XII.

† This Prince, having quarrelled with his father, fled, and took refuge at the court of Persia. Vide Universal History, Vol. XII.

conference, his Majesty observed, "As it is not customary for the Othmān princes to send ambassadors to foreign courts, how does it happen that the Grand Signior has now sent you, a pious Mussulmān, on this business?" * The answer which Sinān Beg gave to this question was a very sensible one, and much approved. He observed that it certainly was contrary to their customs to send ambassadors to strangers; but as the strictest intimacy and friendship now subsisted between the two States, and all animosity and jealousy was perfectly eradicated, an exchange of embassies between such friends was by no means inconsistent with their rules and regulations. His Majesty applauded the speaker, and said,—

POETRY:

The abilities of the messenger discover the judgment of the master.

After the return of Sinān Beg, two ambassadors of the Grand Signior,† viz. Aly Pāshā and Hussen Aghā, arrived, attended by an escort of 300, and having in their train altogether 708 persons. They were honoured the first day by an audience in the garden of Sâādet Abād, when they presented a letter, replete with expressions of friendship, written entirely by Soleymān himself.

On the second day they were again honoured by an audience at the palace, when they delivered their presents, consisting of various valuable and curious articles; such as, instruments and vessels inlaid with gold and precious stones, daggers, scymitars, cloths of different kinds, and rarities from the several countries of Europe. All these articles were displayed to the royal view, in front of the lofty gallery of the palace, called the *Chehel Situn* (Forty Pillars). His Majesty, having (some time after) conferred honours on all the members of the embassy according to their respective ranks, gave them their audience of leave.‡

* Soleymān wrote, with his own hand, a postscript to the public letter; in which he gave Shāh Tahmāsp the option, either to deliver up his son to the ambassador, or to put out his eyes; both of which demands the Shāh considered as disgraceful to all parties.

† The general adoption of this title has induced me to use it, although it is not a translation of any of the Turkish Emperor's titles.

‡ It is related, in the Twelfth Volume of the Universal History, that the Turkish Prince was given up to these ambassadors; but our author postpones this disgraceful event until the third embassy.

In the year of the Hejira 969, (A. D. 1561,) Khosrau Pāshā, a person of the highest rank among the Othmāns, accompanied by Aly Aghā Capūjy Bāshī, arrived, and presented letters, written in the most friendly and conciliatory style, from the Emperor Soleymān. The consequences of this embassy have been related in our account of the Prince Bāyezīd.* After this a fourth embassy, at the head of which was Asbeg Beg, a confidential person of the Grand Signior's, arrived at the Heavenly Court, bringing with him numerous presents from the Turkish Emperor for his Majesty of Persia. The most valuable of these were, forty Syrian and Arabian horses, each of which rivalled the others in goodness and swiftness. Every horse bore a saddle studded with gold, silver, and precious stones, and covered with housings of embroidered cloth. There was also the sum of 500,000 *Falory*† ashrafies, equal, in the currency of Persia, to 50,000 royal Irāky tōmāns,‡ besides various rarities and curiosities; the *whole* of which his Majesty, whose generous mind is as capacious as the ocean, distributed amongst the princes, nobles, governors, and officers, according to their respective ranks; excepting some articles which he sent to different princes; viz. to the Uzbeg chiefs; to Pīr Mohammed Khān, of Balkh; to Abd Allah Khān, of Bokhārā; to Abu Sāēd Khān, of Khūārizm; and to Abūl Mohammed Khān, and Jājim Khān, of Urgenj. He also sent a portion of the Othmān presents to his mother.§

After the death of Soleymān, and the accession of Sultān Selīm (the Second) to all his father's dominions, this Prince, in the year 975, (A.D. 1567,) sent a splendid embassy, under Mohammed Aghā, to the court of Cazvīn. The letter which he brought was written in the most affectionate terms, and in the style of a dutiful son to his father. The subject of it was, soliciting a confirmation and renewal of the treaty of peace, and assurances of eternal

* The Prince and his four sons were delivered up to the ambassadors, by whom they were shamefully murdered. Our author attempts to palliate this disgraceful action, by saying the Persian King did not suspect such conduct; and that if he had not given up the Prince, a war would have ensued, and thousands of Mussulmāns lost their lives.

† Probably Florins.

‡ A Tōmān is worth fifteen dollars and a half.

§ Shāh Tahmāsp probably considered these presents as "the price of blood," and either unlawful or unlucky to be kept by himself.

ORIENTAL TRANSLATION FUND

OF

GREAT BRITAIN AND IRELAND.

Patron:

His Most Excellent Majesty
KING WILLIAM THE FOURTH.

Vice-Patrons:

His Majesty the KING of the BELGIANS.
His Royal Highness the DUKE of SUSSEX.
His Royal Highness the DUKE of CAMBRIDGE.
His Royal Highness the DUKE of GLOUCESTER.
His Grace the LORD ARCHBISHOP of CANTERBURY.
The Right Honourable the LORD HIGH CHANCELLOR.
His Grace the DUKE of WELLINGTON.
The Most Noble the MARQUESS of LANSDOWNE.
The Right Honourable the EARL SPENCER.
The Right Honourable the EARL AMHERST, late Governor-General of India.
The Right Honourable LORD W. H. C. BENTINCK, G.C.B., Governor-General of India.
The Right Honourable LORD VISCOUNT MELVILLE.
The Right Honourable LORD VISCOUNT GODERICH.
The Right Honourable LORD GRENVILLE, Chancellor of the University of Oxford.
The Right Honourable LORD ELLENBOROUGH, late President of the Board of Commissioners for the Affairs of India.
The Right Honourable C. W. WILLIAMS WYNN, M.P., President of the Royal Asiatic Society of Great Britain and Ireland.
The Right Honourable SIR ROBERT PEEL, Bart., M.P.
The Right Honourable HENRY GOULBURN, M.P.
The Right Honourable S. R. LUSHINGTON, Governor of Madras.
Lieutenant General SIR E. BARNES, K.C.B., late Governor of Ceylon.
Major-General SIR JOHN MALCOLM, G.C B., late Governor of Bombay.
H. T. COLEBROOKE, Esq., Director of the Royal Asiatic Society of Great Britain and Ireland.

Officers.

Chairman:

The Right Honourable Sir Gore Ouseley, Bart., Vice-President R.A.S., F.R.S. &c. &c. &c.

Deputy-Chairmen:

The Right Honourable the Earl of Munster, Vice-President R.A.S., F.R.S, &c. &c. &c.
The Right Honourable Sir E. H. East, Bart., M.P., F.R.S., &c. &c. &c.
The Right Honourable C. W. W. Wynn, M.P., F.R S., President R.A.S., &c. &c. &c.
Sir G. T. Staunton, Bart., M.P., V.P.R.A.S., F.R.S., &c. &c. &c.
Sir A. Johnston, V.P.R.A.S., F.R.S., &c. &c. &c.

Auditor, J. B. S. Morritt, Esq., F.S.A.

Treasurer, The Right Honourable the Earl of Munster.

Honorary Secretary, Graves C. Haughton, Esq., M.A., F.R.S., &c. &c. &c.

Honorary Foreign Secretary, Frederick Augustus Rosen, Ph. D.

It is requested that those Individuals or Institutions who are willing to subscribe to the Oriental Translation Fund, will send their names, addressed to "the Secretary, Royal Asiatic Society's House, No. 14, Grafton-street, Bond-street, London;" and inform him where their subscriptions will be paid. Subscriptions will also be received by the Branch Committees at Calcutta, Madras, and Rome.

LIST OF WORKS

PRINTED FOR

THE ORIENTAL TRANSLATION FUND.

AND SOLD BY

Mr. Murray, Messrs. Parbury, Allen, and Co., and Mr. Straker, London; Messrs. Thacker and Co., Calcutta; Messrs. Binny and Co., Madras; Messrs. Leckie and Co., Bombay; Treuttel and Würtz, and Messrs. De Bure frères, Paris; and Ernest Fleischer, Leipzig.

N.B. The Title-pages of all works printed for the Fund are ornamented with a Vignette, bearing the motto "Ex Oriente Lux."

1.

THE TRAVELS OF IBN BATUTA,

Translated from the abridged Arabic Manuscript Copies preserved in the Public Library of Cambridge, with NOTES, illustrative of the History, Geography, Botany, Antiquities, &c. occurring throughout the Work.
By the Rev. S. LEE, B.D., Professor of Hebrew in the University of Cambridge, &c. &c.
In Demy Quarto; price £1.

2.

MEMOIRS OF THE EMPEROR JAHANGUEIR,

Written by Himself, and translated from a Persian Manuscript,
By MAJOR DAVID PRICE, of the Bombay Army, &c. &c.
In Demy Quarto; 12s.

3.

THE TRAVELS OF MACARIUS, PATRIARCH OF ANTIOCH,

Written by his attendant Archdeacon, Paul of Aleppo, in Arabic.
Part the First.—Anatolia, Romelia, and Moldavia.
Translated by F. C. BELFOUR, A.M. Oxon. &c. &c.
In Demy Quarto; 10s.
For Part II. of this Work—see No. 14.

4.

HAN KOONG TSEW, or THE SORROWS OF HAN,

A Chinese Tragedy, translated from the Original, with Notes, and a Specimen of the Chinese Text. By JOHN FRANCIS DAVIS, F.R.S., &c.
In Demy Quarto; 5s.

5.

HISTORY OF THE AFGHANS,

Translated from the Persian of Neamet Allah. Part I.
By BERNHARD DORN, Ph. D., &c.
In Demy Quarto; 14s.

6.

THE FORTUNATE UNION,

A Romance, translated from the Chinese Original, with Notes and Illustrations; to which is added, a Chinese Tragedy.
By JOHN FRANCIS DAVIS, F.R.S., &c.
Two Vols. Demy 8vo.; 16s.

7.

YAKKUN NATTANNAWA,

A Cingalese Poem, descriptive of the Ceylon System of Demonology; to which is appended the Practices of a Capua or Devil Priest, as described by a Budhist: and KOLAN NATTANNAWA, a Cingalese Poem, descriptive of the Characters assumed by Natives of Ceylon in a Masquerade.
Illustrated with Plates from Cingalese Designs.
Translated by JOHN CALLAWAY, late Missionary in Ceylon.
In Demy Octavo; 8s.

8.

THE ADVENTURES OF HATIM TAI,

A Romance, translated from the Persian. By DUNCAN FORBES, A.M.
In Demy Quarto; 16s.

9.

THE LIFE OF SHEIKH MOHAMMED ALI HAZIN,

Written by Himself: translated from two Persian Manuscripts, and Illustrated with Notes explanatory of the History, Poetry, Geography, &c. which therein occur.
By F. C. BELFOUR, M.A. Oxon. &c. &c.
In Demy Octavo; 10s. 6d.
For the Persian Text of this Work—see No. 16.

10.

MEMOIRS OF A MALAYAN FAMILY,

Written by themselves; and translated from the Original,
By W. MARSDEN, F.R.S., &c. &c.
In Demy Octavo; 2s. 6d.

11.

HISTORY OF THE WAR IN BOSNIA,

During the Years 1737-8 and 9.

Translated from the Turkish by C. FRASER, Professor of German in the Naval and Military Academy, Edinburgh. In Demy Octavo; 4s.

12.

THE MULFŪZAT TIMURY; or AUTOBIOGRAPHICAL MEMOIRS OF THE MOGHUL EMPEROR TIMŪR,

Written in the Jagtay Turky language, turned into Persian by Abú Tálib Hussaini, and translated into English

By MAJOR CHARLES STEWART, late Professor of Oriental Languages in the Honourable East-India Company's College.

With a Map of Transoxania. In Demy Quarto; 12s.

13.

THE HISTORY OF VARTAN AND OF THE BATTLE OF THE ARMENIANS,

Containing an Account of the Religious Wars between the Persians and Armenians, by Elisæus Bishop of the Amadunians.

Translated from the Armenian, by C. F. NEUMANN,

Member of the Armenian Academy of the Mechitaristes at St. Lazaro, &c. &c.

In Demy Quarto; 10s.

14.

THE TRAVELS OF MACARIUS, PATRIARCH OF ANTIOCH,

Written by his Attendant Archdeacon Paul of Aleppo, in Arabic.

Part the Second.—Wallachia, Moldavia, and the Cossack Country.

Translated by F. C. BELFOUR, A.M. Oxon. &c. &c.

In Demy Quarto; 10s.

For the First Part of this Work—see No. 3.

15.

THE LIFE OF HAFIZ UL MULK, HAFIZ REHMUT KHAN.

Written by his Son Nawáb Must'ujáb Khán Buhadar, and entitled Gulistán-i Rehmut.

Abridged and translated from the Persian, by CHARLES ELLIOTT, Esq., Of the Bengal Civil Service.

In Demy 8vo; 5s.

16.

THE LIFE OF SHEIKH MOHAMMED ALI HAZIN,

Written by Himself; edited from two Persian Manuscripts, and noted with their various Readings, by F. C. BELFOUR, M.A. Oxon, &c. &c.

In Demy 8vo. 10s. 6d.

For the English Translation of this Work—see No. 9.

17.

MISCELLANEOUS TRANSLATIONS FROM ORIENTAL LANGUAGES,

Volume the First. In Demy 8vo. 8s.

CONTENTS:

I. Notes of a Journey into the Interior of Northern Africa.—By Haj Ibn-ud-din Al-Aghwaati. Translated from the Arabic by W. B. Hodgson, Esq., late American Consul at Algiers, F.M.R.A.S.

II. Extracts from the Sakaa Thevan Saasteram, or Book of Fate.—Translated from the Tamul Language, by the Rev. Joseph Roberts, Cor. M.R.A.S.

III. The Last Days of Krishna and the Sons of Pandu, from the concluding Section of the Mahabharat. Translated from the Persian version, made by Nekkeib Khan, in the time of the Emperor Akbar. By Major David Price, of the Bombay Army, M.R.A.S., of the Oriental Translation Committee, and of the Royal Society of Literature.

IV. The Vedala Cadai, being the Tamul Version of a Collection of Ancient Tales in the Sanscrit Language; popularly known throughout India, and entitled the Vetála Panchavinsati. Translated by B. G. Babington, M.D., F.R.S., M.R.A.S., M. Madras Lit. Soc., &c.

V. Indian Cookery, as practised and described by the Natives of the East. Translated by Sandford Arnot.

18.

THE ALGEBRA OF MOHAMMED BEN MUSA, ARABIC AND ENGLISH.

Edited and translated by FREDERIC ROSEN.

In Demy Octavo; 8s.

19.

THE HISTORY OF THE MARITIME WARS OF THE TURKS,

Translated from the Turkish of Haji Khalifeh, by JAMES MITCHELL.

Part I. In Demy Quarto; 7s.

20.

TRANSLATIONS FROM THE CHINESE AND ARMENIAN,

By CHARLES F. NEUMANN.

In Demy 8vo. 12s. bds.

CONTENTS:

I. History of the Pirates who infested the China Sea, from 1807 to 1810. Translated from the Chinese Original, with Notes and Illustrations.

II. The Catechism of the Shamans; or, the Laws and Regulations of the Priesthood of Buddha, in China. Translated from the Chinese Original, with Notes and Illustrations.

III. Vahram's Chronicle of the Armenian Kingdom in Cilicia, during the time of the Crusades. Translated from the Original Armenian, with Notes and Illustrations.

21.

THE GEOGRAPHICAL WORKS OF SÀDIK ISFAHÀNI'.

Translated by J. C. from Original Persian MSS. in the Collection of Sir William Ouseley, the Editor.

Octavo.

22.

THE SHÀH NÀMEH OF THE PERSIAN POET FIRDAUSI'.

Translated and Abridged in Prose and Verse, with Notes and Illustrations, By JAMES ATKINSON, Esq.,

Of the Honourable East-India Company's Bengal Medical Service.

Octavo.

23.

THE TEZKEREH AL VAKIAT; OR, PRIVATE MEMOIRS OF THE MOGHUL EMPEROR HUMAYUN.

Written in the Persian Language by Jouher, a Confidential Domestic of his Majesty.

Translated by Major CHARLES STEWART, of the Honourable East-India Company's Service, M.R.A.S., &c. &c.

Quarto.

24.

THE SIYAR-UL-MUTAKHERIN,

A History of the Mahomedan Power in India, during the last Century.

By MIR GHOLAM HUSSEIN-KHAN.

Revised from the Translation of Haji Mustafa, and Collated with the Persian Original, by Lieut. Colonel John Briggs, M.R.A.S. &c. &c.

Vol. I. 8vo.

25.

HOEÏ LAN KI; OU, L'HISTOIRE DU CERCLE DE CRAIE,

Drame en prose et en vers, traduit du Chinois, et accompagné de notes,

Par Stanislas Julien. 8vo.

26.

SAN KOKF TSOU RAN TO SETS; OU, APERCU GENERAL DES TROIS ROYAUMES.

Traduit de l'Original Japonais-Chinois, par M. J. KLAPROTH.

(Ouvrage accompagné de cinque Cartes.)

Octavo.

27.

A HISTORY OF THE EARLY KINGS OF PERSIA,

Commencing with Kaiomars, the first of the Peshdádian Dynasty, terminating with the Death of Dárá, and the Conquest of Irán by Alexander the Great.

Translated from the Persian History of Mirkhond, entitled "Rauzat-us-Saffá,"

By DAVID SHEA,

Of the Oriental Department in the Honourable East-India Company's College.

Octavo.

28.

ANNALS OF THE TURKISH EMPIRE, FROM 1591 TO 1659 OF THE CHRISTIAN ERA.

Translated from the Turkish, by CHARLES FRASER.

29.

A CRITICAL ESSAY ON VARIOUS MANUSCRIPT WORKS, ARABIC AND PERSIAN.

Translated by J. C. from an original Persian MS. in the possession of Sir William Ouseley, the Editor. 8vo.

30.

RAGHUVANSA, KÀLIDÀSÆ CARMEN,

Sanskrite et Latine

Edidit ADOLPHUS FRIDERICUS STENZLER

LIST OF WORKS IN THE PRESS.

The Travels of Evliya Effendi; translated by M. de Hammer.
This work contains an account in Turkish, of the travels of Evliya in all parts of the Turkish empire, and in Turkestan, &c. in the middle of the seventeenth century.

Nipon u dai itsi ran; translated by M. Jules de Klaproth.
This Japanese work contains the History of the Dairis or Ecclesiastical Emperors of Japan from the year 660 Ante Christum.

The Fo koue ke, translated by M. Abel Rémusat.
This very curious Chinese work contains an account of the travels of some Buddhist Priests, during the years 399-411 A.D. from the city of Si ngan fu in China, through Tartary, Hindoostan, Ceylon, &c., and greatly elucidates the ancient geography and religion of Central Asia and India. It will likewise be illustrated by the learned translator from many original Chinese writers.

A History of Morocco; translated by Walter Price, Esq.
An Arabic work containing a history of the establishment of the Mohammedan power in the Barbary States, and in Spain, from the eighth to the fourteenth century.

The great Geographical Work of Idrísí; translated by the Rev. G. C. Renouard, B.D.
This Arabic work was written A.D. 1153, to illustrate a large silver globe made for Roger, King of Sicily, and is divided into the seven climates described by the Greek geographers.

The Travels of Macarius, Patriarch of Antioch. Written by his Attendant Archdeacon Paul of Aleppo; translated by F. C. Belfour, Esq. M.A., LL.D, Part III.
This Arabic Manuscript, which is of great rarity, describes the Patriarch's journey through Syria, Anatolia, Rumelia, Walachia, Moldavia, and Russia, between the years 1650 and 1660 of the Christian Æra.

Hájí Khalífa's Bibliographical Dictionary; translated by Monsieur Gustav Flugel.
This valuable Arabic work, which formed the ground-work of d'Herbelot's "Bibliothèque Oriental," contains accounts of upwards of 13,000 Arabic, Persian, and Turkish works, arranged alphabetically.

LIST OF TRANSLATIONS PREPARING FOR PUBLICATION.

Class 1st.—Theology, Ethics, and Metaphysics.

The Sánkhya Káriká; translated by Henry Thomas Colebrooke, Esq.
This Sanscrit work contains, in seventy-two stanzas, the principles of the Sánkhya System of Metaphysical Philosophy.

The Li ki, translated by M. Stanislas Julien.
This ancient Chinese work, which is attributed to Confucius, was the original moral and ceremonial code of China, and is still the principal authority on those subjects in that empire.

A Collation of the Syriac MSS. of the New Testament, both Nestorian and Jacobite, that are accessible in England, by the Rev. Professor Lee.
This collation will include the various readings of the Syriac MSS. of the New Testament in the British Museum, and the Libraries at Oxford, Cambridge, &c.

The Didascalia, or Apostolical Constitutions of the Abyssinian Church; translated by T. P. Platt, Esq. A.M.
This ancient Ethiopic work is unknown in Europe, and contains many very curious opinions.

The Vrihad Aranyaka; translated by Dr. Stenzler.
This ancient Sanscrit Upanishad is reckoned part of the Yajur Veda. It consists of reflections and dialogues on the origin and nature of the gods, men, fire, &c., and is one of the principal authorities in the Vedanta system of philosophy.

The Akhlák-i-Násirí, of Násir-ud-din of Tús in Bokharia; translated by the Rev. H. G. Keene, A.M.
This Persian system of Ethics is an elaborate composition, formed on Greek models, and is very highly esteemed in Persia.

The Harivansa, translated by M. Langlois.
This Sanscrit work is generally considered as a Supplement to the Mahábhárata, and throws much light upon Hindu Mythology.

Class 2d.—History, Geography, and Travels.

The Sharaf Námah; translated by Professor Charmoy.
This is a Persian History of the Dynasties which have governed in Kurdistan, written by Sheref Ibn Shams-ud-din, at the close of the sixteenth century.

The History of Mázindarán and Tabaristán; translated by Professor Charmoy.
This is a Persian history of part of the Persian empire, written by Zahir-uddin, and comes down to A.D. 1475.

The Tárikh-i-Afghán; translated by Professor Bernhard Dorn. Part II.
This is a Persian History of the Afghans, who claim to be descended from the Jews. It will be accompanied by an account of the Afghan tribes.

The Annals of Elias, Metropolitan of Nisibis; translated by the Rev. Josiah Forshall, A.M.
This Syriac Chronicle contains chronological tables of the principal dynasties of the world, brief memoirs of the Patriarchs of the Nestorian church, and notices of the most remarkable events in the East, from the birth of our Saviour to the beginning of the eleventh century.

Ibn Haukal's Geography; translated by Professor Hamaker.
This Arabic work was compiled in the 10th century by a celebrated Mohammedan Traveller, and is not the same as the Oriental Geography of Ebn Haukal that was translated by Sir William Ouseley.

The History of Rájá Krishan Chandra, translated by G. C. Haughton, Esq., M.A. F.R.S., &c. &c.
This Bengali work includes an account of the Rise of the Raja's family, of the events that led to the fatal catastrophe of the Black Hole at Calcutta, and of the triumphant establishment of the English under Lord Clive in Bengal.

The Chronicle of Abulfat'h Ibn Abulhasan Alsamari; translated by the Rev. T. Jarrett, M.A.
This rare Arabic work, of which only one perfect copy is known to be in Europe, is a History of the Samaritans from the creation to the middle of the fourteenth century.

Ibn Khaldún's History of the Berbers; translated by the Rev. Professor Lee.
This is a most rare and valuable work, containing an account of the origin, progress, and decline of the dynasties which governed the northern coast of Africa.

Ibn Koteiba's History of the Arabians, translated by Dr. J. H. Moeller.
This celebrated work contains the History of the Arabians from the time of Ismael the son of Abraham to near the end of the third century of the Mahommedan, or the 9th of the Christian era.

Makrizi's Khitat, or History and Statistics of Egypt; translated by Abraham Salamé, Esq.
This Arabic work includes accounts of the conquest of Egypt by the Caliphs, A.D. 640; and of the cities, rivers, ancient and modern inhabitants of Egypt, &c.

A History of the Birman Empire, translated by Father Sangermano.
This work, which contains the political and religious history of Birmah, was translated by Father Sangermano, who was a missionary in Ava twenty-six years. It also furnishes accounts of the natural productions, laws, and metaphysics of that country.

The Tuhfat al Kibár of Háji Khalífah; translated by Mr. James Mitchell. Part II.
This Turkish History contains an account of the maritime wars of the Turks in the Mediterranean and Black Seas, and on the Danube, &c., principally in the time of the Crusades.

The Siyar ul Mutakherin of Mír Gholâm Hussein Khan; translated by Lieut. Col. John Briggs. Vol. II.
This celebrated Persian work comprises the annals of Hindustán from the time of the Emperor Aurungzebe to the administration of Warren Hastings in Bengal.

The Khatai Nameh; translated by M. Fleischer.
This curious Turkish work contains a description of China, with accounts of its government, laws, &c.

The Tarikh Tabari; translated by M. Dubeux.
A highly esteemed and very authentic history, written in Persian, containing accounts of the Patriarchs, Prophets, Philosophers, of Mohammed and of the Khalifs.

Class 3d.—Bibliography, Belles-Lettres, and Biography.

Haft Paiker, an historical Romance of Bahrám Gúr; translated by the Right Hon. Sir Gore Ouseley, Bart.
This Persian poem of Nazami of Ganjah, contains the romantic history of Bahrám, the Vth of the Sassanian dynasty of Persian Kings.

Mihr-u-Mushteri; translated by the Right Hon. Sir Gore Ouseley, Bart.
This Persian Poem, of which an abridgment will be published, was composed by Muhammed Assár, and celebrates the friendship and adventures of Mihr and Mushteri, the sons of King Shapur and his grand Vizier.

Ibn Khallikán's Lives of Illustrious Men: translated by Dr. F. A. Rosen.
This is an Arabic Biographical Dictionary, arranged alphabetically, of the most celebrated Arabian historians, poets, warriors, &c. who lived in the seven first centuries of the era of Mahommed, A.D. 600 to A.D. 1300.

The Bustán of Sádi; translated by James Ross, Esq., A.M.
This is a much-admired Persian Poem, consisting of Tales, &c. illustrative of moral duties.

The Divan of the Huzeilis; translated by Professor Kosegarten.
This is a collection of ancient Arabic Poems similar to the Hamasa; the translation will be accompanied by the Arabic Text and scholia.

Royal Asiatic Society's House,
14, *Grafton Street, Bond Street, London.*
1st June 1832.